W. K Tweedie

Glad Tidings

Or, the gospel of peace. A series of daily meditations for Christian disciples

W. K Tweedie

Glad Tidings
Or, the gospel of peace. A series of daily meditations for Christian disciples

ISBN/EAN: 9783337222161

Printed in Europe, USA, Canada, Australia, Japan

Cover: Foto ©Lupo / pixelio.de

More available books at **www.hansebooks.com**

GLAD TI[DINGS]

OR,

THE GOSPEL O[F ...]

A

SERIES OF DAILY M[EDITATIONS]

FOR

CHRISTIAN DISC[IPLES]

BY

W. K. TWEED[IE]

WITH AN INTRODUC[TION]

BY H. L. HAST[INGS]

BOSTON:
COPYRIGHT, '84.
H. L. HASTINGS,
SCRIPTURAL TRACT REPOSITORY,
47 CORNHILL.

WORKS BY W. K. TWEEDIE, D.D.

Of the Free Tolbooth Church, Edinburg. 3 vols. Uniform in size and style of binding.

GLAD TIDINGS; or the Gospel of Peace. A series of meditations for Christian Disciples. With a preface by H. L. Hastings. 75 cts.

A LAMP TO THE PATH: or the Word of God in the Heart, the Home, the Workshop and the Market-place. With an introduction by H. L. Hastings; 75 cts.

SEED-TIME AND HARVEST: or Sow Well and Reap Well. A Book for the Young. With a preface by H. L. Hastings. 75 cts.

₊ *Address all orders to H. L. HASTINGS, 47 Cornhill, Boston.*

INTRODUCTION.

The grandest event in human history was announced by an angel, saying; "Behold I bring you Good Tidings of great joy, which shall be to all people." The beginning of the gospel was an outburst of triumphant song from all the host of heaven; and the term gospel, or *Good Tidings*, fitly describes the message which God has sent to scatter brightness through a dark and desolate world, which makes glad the hearts of the weary and the disconsolate on earth, and which, when re-echoed to the skies, causes joy in heaven over sinners returning to the Lord. The world without the gospel would be a world of darkness. The highest joys of social and domestic life, the songs we sing, the praises we offer, and the prayers in which we pour our sorrows at a Saviour's feet, all have their birth in "the glorious gospel of the blessed God."

This gospel is a message of peace, peace to them that are afar off in the dark wilderness of sin and sorrow; and peace to them that are nigh, "who have been "brought nigh by the blood of Christ," and have been made partakers of the riches of Divine favor, and enabled to rejoice with joy unspeakable, and full of glory.

The work of righteousness is peace; and when the righteousness of God is revealed in the gospel, it commences its peaceful work for man. First there is "Peace *with* God, through our Lord Jesus Christ." The days of rebellion are ended, the soul accepts the amnesty which God has offered, and returns to that allegiance from which fallen man has so deeply revolted. The rebellious strife is over; and though there may be tumult in the world without, and conflict in the heart within, yet there is calm above, there is peace *with* God. The soul, freed from the disorder of rebellion, and yielding to the mild and beneficent sway of its Creator, falls into a sweet and hallowed harmony with Him who ruleth the earth and heaven, and who worketh all things according to the counsel of his will. When once peace is made with God, then His peace enshrines itself within the obedient heart. The conflict being over, and the obdurate will bowed in submission, the weapons of rebellion are laid down, the Holy Spirit of God is shed forth within the heart, and the fruits of that Spirit, which are "love, joy and peace," are brought forth in their season. From that time the trusting child of God is held as by a hallowed spell. The world may rage, storms may rise, thunders may roll, tempests burst, and billows swell outside, but there is peace within.

Seamen tell us, that sometimes, when ships are in peril from storms, a tiny stream of *oil*, poured over the vessel's side, will spread over acres of tumultuous water, quieting and calming the furious waves, so that "in the midst of the raging sea the vessel rides securely within that charmed circle over which the oil has spread." So the peace of God, dwelling in the heart, overflows, and thus there is peace at home, peace in the family, peace in the community, peace amid the turmoil of worldly care and strife, peace in the fellowship of the saints of God, peace which causes the perturbed and despairing world to look with astonishment upon the calmness of the trusting saint, peace which is to the unsaved an insoluble mystery, —the peace of God that passeth knowledge,—the peace that passeth all understanding.

The gospel of peace has blessed the world for ages. It has beaten swords into plough-shares and spears into pruning-hooks. It has caused the warrior to lay down his weapons, and the man of blood to become a man of peace and love. And though heathenish barbarism still prevails, arrogating to itself the profession of Christianity until the name of God is blasphemed among the heathen through the wickedness of the sinful nations and peoples of Christendom, yet wherever the *true gospel* has gone, there it has ever been a message of peace to man.

But we must distinguish between "the *gospel* of peace," and the peace itself which that gospel proclaims. As "the gospel of the kingdom" is the good news of the kingdom, but it is *not* the kingdom in its fullness; so the gospel of peace, with all its blessed present fruits, is but the proclamation and promise of greater peace and grander blessing than the world has ever known.

That Holy Child who was born in Bethlehem bears the titles, Wonderful, Counsellor, Mighty God, Everlasting Father, Prince of Peace. Isa. ix. Wonderful in his birth, and in the mystery of his divine existence; a Counsellor such as the world had never known before, his counsels have for many centuries blessed a race which had long wandered in perplexity and darkness. He is Mighty God, mighty to save, mighty to pardon, mighty to redeem, mighty to heal, mighty to hush the winds and calm the waves, mighty to rebuke demons, conquer the powers of darkness, and burst the fetters of the tomb; mighty as the bearer of all power in heaven and in earth, which is given into his hands, while he sits at the right hand of God, expecting until his enemies be made his footstool. He is the everlasting Father; Father of eternal ages yet unborn, Father of that race which it was predicted that he should behold when, risen from the grave, he should see his seed, and prolong his days; Father of the deathless multitudes who, having relinquished the life derived from the first Adam, lay hold on that life eternal which comes through the Second Man, the Lord from heaven, and whom he shall present in the presence of the glory of the Father, saying, "Behold, I and the children whom thou hast given me."

But he is the Prince of peace, bringing peace as

God's message to a lost world; preaching peace to the troubled and the tempest-tossed; making peace through the blood of his cross; and finally making wars to cease to the ends of the earth, breaking the bow, and cutting the spear in sunder, and burning the chariot in the fire; scattering the nations that delight in war; breaking the rebellious as with a rod of iron, and dashing them in pieces like a potter's vessel; overcoming every foe, until death, the last enemy, is destroyed. And when all things are subdued unto Him; and the mountains shall bring peace to the people, and the little hills, by righteousness; when there shall be abundance of peace so long as the moon endureth; when the God of peace shall bruise Satan under the feet of his saints, and glory, and honor, and peace shall be given to every man that worketh good;—when we shall enter upon those coming cycles of eternal bliss and gladness, we shall know the meaning of that last resplendent title, "Prince of peace," and shall comprehend as never before, "how beautiful upon the mountains are the feet of him that bringeth good tidings, that publisheth *peace;* that bringeth good news of good, that publisheth salvation, that saith unto Zion, Thy God reigneth!" Isa. lii. 7.

To those who in the midst of this troubled and disordered world would seek peace and pursue it; to those who long to share the Wonders of Redeeming Love, and who commit themselves to the guidance of the Shepherd of Israel, these pages are commended, in the hope that they will bring comfort to troubled and tempest-tossed souls, and guide the feet of weary wanderers "in the way of peace."

H. L. H.

Boston, Mass., July, 1884.

PREFACE.

Religion may be contemplated under various aspects:

First, It may be viewed as it existed in man's soul when he was first created. A principle of veneration towards the Supreme was then implanted in his nature; and we can no more escape from its influence than from any of the great laws which should regulate man's conduct. Religion in that aspect, however, is now seen only as a defaced and distorted thing. It is held by Atheists, in spite of all their denials of a God — by Deists — and by heathens.

Secondly, Religion may be viewed as it is revealed and recorded in the Book of Inspiration — "the Word of the Lord, which endureth for ever."

Thirdly, It may be contemplated, as it is often embodied in a series of doctrines, which are intellectually believed upon sufficient evidence, as men believe historical or moral truths; and this is the form of religion which satisfies many of the cultivated minds of Christendom. It is not a life — a principle of action, extending to all that has reference to man's responsibility to God — but a theory, a system, a creed — as unlike the warm realities of truth, as the ice palace of the Northern Empress was unlike the ordinary dwellings of men.

Or *finally,* Religion may be viewed as *taught to an individual soul by the Holy Spirit, according to the Inspired Book.* It then regulates the life; it purifies the heart; it animates our hopes; it points our thoughts to God; it is the means of re-connecting us with the Eternal, and preparing us for glory, through Him who is the sum and the centre of all saving truth — the Son of God. In this form, religion appears in its highest manifestation as *Devotion,* or communion with God, according to his Word; and when it has advanced to this stage, it becomes next of kin to glory, honour, and immortality, whether it be presiding over the activities of life, purifying and hallowing its joys, or directing the aspirations of the lonely soul when it is "feeling after God," and a sense of his favor.

The following brief Meditations are designed to foster godliness of the last-mentioned type. The Inspired Word is at once the standard and the substance of all that is true in regard to salvation; and for that reason, the conscience, the heart, and soul, are here kept in close contact with the truth which the Holy Spirit inspired Nothing systematic, as an exhibition of truth, has been here attempted, though the three sections of the volume bear reference to the three stages in which personal religion may be studied: or, first, As *presented* — " Good Tidings;" secondly, As *attracting* the soul by its " Wonders;" and thirdly, As *realized*, when man is under the gracious guardianship of " the Shepherd of Israel."

Ours is a restless age. The truth of God is now in danger of being exiled from the mind by the engrossments and agitations amid which we live. But would men be kept steadfast and unmovable? Would they be preserved from pining in their religion, like an exotic in a chilling climate? Then, amid their cares, their journeyings, and their spiritual perils, let the soul be at once defended and refreshed by communion with the God of the Word. In simplicity and earnestness of spirit, let at least a crumb of the bread of life be tasted, when we cannot be satisfied to the full. The world will then be more under our feet, and heaven more in our heart; and it is to promote that result, by the blessing of the Spirit, that these Meditations upon some views of the gospel of His grace, are offered to as many as have learned to " call on the name of the Lord."

CONTENTS.

The Gospel of Peace.

		Page
THE WAYS OF MAN,	Eccles. vii. 29,	13
THE FOUNTAIN OF HOPE,	Gen. iii. 15,	16
THE OPEN FOUNTAIN,	Isaiah i. 18,	18
THE ALMIGHTY ADVOCATE,	Heb. vii. 25,	20
GOOD TIDINGS OF GREAT JOY,	Luke ii. 10,	22
LOVE FROM GOD AND TO HIM,	Rom. v. 8,	24
THE COMPASSIONATE ONE,	Isaiah xlii. 3,	26
REDEMPTION COMPLETE,	John xix. 30,	28
SALVATION FREE,	Isaiah lv. 1,	30
THE RIGHTEOUSNESS OF GOD,	Isaiah xlvi. 13,	32
THE SPIRIT OF JESUS,	1 Cor. xii. 3,	34
THE BLOOD OF CHRIST,	Jer. i. 20,	36
THE GOD OF PARDONS,	Isaiah xliii. 25,	38
ON EARTH PEACE,	Luke ii. 14,	40
THE GLORIOUS GOSPEL,	Rom. v. 6,	42
GRACE ABOUNDING,	Mark xvi. 15,	44
THE ALMIGHTY PROMISER,	Isaiah liv. 10,	46
THE WAY TO THE FATHER,	John xiv. 6,	48

CONTENTS.

		Page
Look and Live,	Isaiah xlv. 22,	50
The Abundance of Peace,	Psalm lxviii. 18,	52
The Price of Redemption,	Isaiah xliv. 22,	54
Gold Tried in the Fire,	Rev. iii. 18,	56
Grace and Glory,	Zech. iv. 7,	58
The Gift of God,	Rom. vi. 23,	60
The Refuge of Lies,	Isaiah xxviii. 15,	62
Faith,	Rom. i. 17.	64
Jehovah our Righteousness,	Jer. xxiii. 6,	66
The New Heart,	John iii. 7,	68
Godly Sorrow,	Zech. xii. 10,	70
Jesus,	Matt. i. 21,	72
The Cross,	Col. i. 20,	74
The Hiding-Place,	Isaiah xxxii. 2,	76
The Sinner's Substitute,	Isaiah liii. 5,	78
The Alternative,	2 Cor. iv. 3, 4,	80
The Force of Truth,	Heb. iv. 12,	82
The Glory of Man,	Isaiah lx. 19,	84
The Sun of Righteousness,	Mal. iv. 2,	86
Spiritual Declension,	John vi. 66,	88
The Great Restoration,	2 Chron. vi. 18,	90
The Heart-Searcher,	Heb. iv. 13,	92
The Arm of the Lord,	Judges viii. 4,	94
The Stronghold,	Numb. xxxiii. 23,	96

The Wonders of Redeeming Love.

		Page
THE WONDERFUL,	Isaiah ix. 6,	100
THE TWO PLEAS,	Psalm xxv. 11,	102
THE REIGN OF LOVE,	2 Cor. v. 14,	104
THE WONDER OF WONDERS,	Luke xviii. 13,	106
THE GOD OF PARDONS,	Micah vii. 18,	108
PARDON AND ITS FRUIT,	2 Sam. xii. 13; Psalm li. 3,	110
ABASED, YET HOPING,	Psalm viii. 4,	112
THE SURE DEFENCE,	Psalm xlvi. 7,	114
THE NAME OF THE LORD,	Exod. xxxiv. 6, 7,	116
THE WISDOM OF GOD,	Rom. xi. 33,	118
HOPE IN GOD,	Psalm xlii. 11,	120
THE PORTION OF THE SOUL,	Psalm xl. 17,	122
A CONTRAST,	Isaiah lv. 8,	124
THE MAN OF SORROWS,	Luke ix. 58,	126
THE BLOOD OF THE CROSS,	Eph. ii. 13,	128
THE MYSTERY OF GODLINESS,	1 Tim. iii. 16,	130
THE GOODLY HERITAGE,	Lam. iii. 24; Deut. xxx. 9,	132
THE BOLDNESS OF FAITH,	Heb. x. 19,	134
THE TRUE AMBITION,	Job xiv. 4,	136
STRENGTH IN WEAKNESS,	2 Cor. xii. 10,	138
THE STAY OF THE SAINT,	Isaiah xxx. 7,	140
THE SPIRIT OF HOLINESS,	1 Cor. iii. 16,	142

CONTENTS.

		Page
The True Forgiveness,	Psalm cxxx. 4,	144
The Believer Complete,	Col. ii. 10,	146
The Right Way,	Psalm cvii. 7,	148
The Glory of Man,	2 Peter i. 4,	150
The Truth Imperishable,	Exod. iii. 2,	152
The Heavenly Witness,	Rom. viii. 16,	154
The Comprehensive Prayer,	Exod. xxxiii. 18,	156
The Obedience of One,	Rom. v. 19,	158
The Message of Peace,	1 John i. 9,	160
Adoption,	1 John iii. 1,	162
The Saviour's Humiliation,	Psalm xxii. 6,	164
Joy in God,	Rom. v. 11,	166
Christ the Life,	Gal. ii. 20,	168
The Curse,	Gal. iii. 13,	170
The Triumph,	Psalm xxiii. 4,	172
Glory,	1 Peter v. 1,	174
The Heart Kept,	Jude 20, 21.	176
Man's Idolatry—The Antidote,	Exod. xxxii. 1,	178
The Destroyer,	1 Peter v. 8,	180
Deliverance from Fear of Death,	Heb. ii. 15,	182
The Heavenly Guide,	Exod. xv. 12,	184
Mercies Deep as Floods,	Deut. xxxii. 11, 12,	186
The Altogether Lovely,	Song v. 10,	188
The Grand Consummation,	1 Cor. ii. 9,	190

CONTENTS.

The Shepherd of Israel.

		Page
THE SHEPHERD OF ISRAEL,	Psalm xxiii. 1,	194
THE FLOCK OF GOD,	Isaiah xliii. 1,	196
THE FAITHFUL PROMISER,	Heb. x. 23,	198
EVERLASTING REMEMBRANCE,	Isaiah xlix. 16,	200
SALVATION MADE SURE,	Heb. xii. 2,	202
THE ALL-SUFFICIENT ONE,	John iv. 29,	204
THE SANCTUARY OF THE SOUL,	Ezek. xl. 16,	206
THE ROCK OF OUR CONFIDENCE,	1 John iv. 4,	208
JOY RESTORED,	Isaiah xii. 1,	210
THE GIFT RECEIVED,	Isaiah xii. 2,	212
STREAMS IN THE DESERT,	Isaiah xii. 3,	214
THE SPIRIT OF PRAISE,	Isaiah xii. 4,	216
SCARCELY SAVED,	1 Peter iv. 18,	218
THE PEACE OF GOD,	Phil. iv. 6, 7,	220
"KNOW THE LORD,"	Hosea vi. 3,	222
THE MYSTERIOUS LIFE,	Col. iii. 3,	224
SORROWING, YET REJOICING,	Isaiah lxiii. 9,	226
THE PATH OF PERIL,	1 Thess. v. 19,	228
THE GREAT CALM,	Matt. xiv. 27,	230
THE THOUGHTS OF VANITY,	Jer. iv. 14,	232
THE EFFECTUAL PRAYER,	Luke xxiii. 42,	234
STRONG IN THE LORD,	Eph. vi. 10,	236

CONTENTS.

		Page
The Lord alone Exalted,	Col. iii. 11,	238
Betrothed for Ever,	Isaiah liv. 5,	240
The Munition of Rocks,	Psalm iii. 6,	242
The Abased Exalted,	Eph. iii. 8,	244
The Great Contrast,	2 Cor. vi. 10,	246
It is Well,	Gen. xlii. 36,	248
The Dew,	Hosea xiv. 5,	250
Prayer: its Power,	Isaiah lxv. 24,	252
The Saviour's Kindred,	Matt. xii. 50,	254
The Hope of Glory,	John vi. 47,	256
The Heavenly-Minded,	Phil. iii. 20,	258
The Crown,	1 John iii. 2,	260
Heavenward Progress,	2 Peter iii. 18,	262
The Second Adam,	1 Cor. xv. 49,	264
Transgression Finished,	Heb. viii. 12,	266
The Triumph,	Phil. i. 23,	268
Death Abolished,	Gen. v. 27,	270
Following the Lamb,	Rev. vii. 17,	272
Heaven,	1 Thess. iv. 14,	274

GLAD TIDINGS;

OR,

THE GOSPEL OF PEACE.

The Ways of Man.

"LO, THIS ONLY HAVE I FOUND, THAT GOD HATH MADE MAN UPRIGHT; BUT THEY HAVE SOUGHT OUT MANY INVENTIONS."— *Eccl.* vii. 29.

THE mere enumeration of these inventions might suffice to lay us in the dust, and cover us with shame and confusion there. A creature once in the image of God, and capable of wearing it again, has consented to forego the use of reason in regard to his soul — to violate the rights of conscience — to deny the righteous claims of the Holy One — to deface his image in man, and show how thorough is the havoc wrought by sin at once in his understanding and his heart.

One of his inventions is to prefer the creature to God — to tremble at the frown, or exult in the smile of the thing made, and utterly disregard its Maker.

Another invention of man's is to expect happiness in sin, the source of all our woe; to rush unwarned along the path which leads to misery, and yet to anticipate blessedness both along the way and at its termination.

Another invention is to repose upon the word of a creature which is the victim of lying vanities, and has a heart which is deceitful above all things, and desperately wicked; and to withhold our confidence from Him who is the truth itself.

And another of our inventions is to prefer existence upon earth to existence in glory; threescore years and ten to eternity; or pleasures which melt into nothing while we try to grasp them, to the joy which is "unspeakable and full of glory."

And another of our inventions is to place our own righteousness before that of God; to repose upon what He declares to be utterly impure, when tested by the standard of heaven, instead of resting upon the everlasting righteousness of the Son of God — the origin of hope to the sons of men.

Or, to name no more, another invention of the fallen creature is to think that the religion which was sufficient in Eden — when no Mediator was needed, for there was no taint of sin — can still suffice when man has become degraded, polluted, and therefore an outcast from the favor of his God.

Now, surely "man's way is his folly" in all such inventions. To be captivated with sin, and to despise holiness — to confide in a creature, and make God a liar — to trample on the claims of conscience, and listen to the voice of passion — to grasp the phantom, and discard the substance; — surely these are proofs sufficient that the image of God has been utterly defaced, when man — responsible, rational, and once God-like man — can thus

"Hate truth, and be the dupe of lies."

But glory to God in the highest — man's primal uprightness may yet be restored. The image of God may be stamped on the soul again. Conscience may be replaced in her supremacy — reason may be made her handmaiden once more — and all may yet move in harmony with the mind of God. Christ is made wisdom to us — behold our folly turned upside down! The Holy Spirit makes all things new — behold the fall and its ruin counteracted by omnipotent grace!

THE PROOF.

"After that, in the wisdom of God, the world by wisdom knew not God, it pleased God by the foolishness of preaching to save them that believe."—1 COR. i. 21.

THE COMPLAINT.

"Frail beauty and false honor are adored,
While Thee they scorn, and trifle with thy Word;
Men heedless pass a Saviour's sorrows by,
And hunt their ruin with a zeal to die."

The Fountain of Hope.

"AND I WILL PUT ENMITY BETWEEN THEE AND THE WOMAN, AND BETWEEN THY SEED AND HER SEED; IT SHALL BRUISE THY HEAD, AND THOU SHALT BRUISE HIS HEEL." — *Gen.* iii. 15.

HERE is the origin at once of anguish and of joy — Of anguish, because man has rebelled against his God; has believed a creature, and made the Creator a liar; has sought happiness in sin, and preferred woe and death to the blessing, and to life. Eden is blighted now; all its beauties are faded, while man's heart is more blighted still. He who is LOVE is now disliked; he is fled from, and dreaded. The whole head is sick, and the whole heart is faint, and that in the very being who lately wore the image of the Holy One.

But here also is the origin of new hope and joy to the fallen — joy from the very God from whom man had turned away, or whom man would not believe — joy, in short, from Him who could not but punish sin, and yet would not but pity the sinner. Here is the first hint of the glad tidings of great joy. Here is the key-note of the Gospel, heard as soon as it was needed, from the lips of Him whose tender mercies are over all his other works. The blessing and the curse, joy and misery, life and death, are here placed side by side. "The seed of the woman shall bruise thy head" — that is the tempter's doom: "Thou shalt bruise his heel" — that is the first prophecy of the Redeemer's woe, and the first glimpse of hope to fallen man. My soul! behold here the loving-kindness of the Lord. Hast thou felt it? Is the heart touched by it? Is this to thee the voice of God indeed; or is it still like an unknown tongue, unfelt, and disregarded? He who discovered the sources of the mighty Nile, tells of his rapture as he gazed upon the fountains. But here is the fountain of that river whose streams make glad the city of our God. Hast thou rejoiced in it? Art thou rejoicing, and preparing to rejoice for ever? O be honest. Be earnest. Is he sane who trifles with his eternity, his soul, and his God — who leaves the great question — where is thy abode for ever to be? — unadjusted, and in doubt!

THE PROOF.

"He that committeth sin is of the devil; for the devil sinneth from the beginning. For this purpose the Son of God was manifested, that he might destroy the works of the devil." — 1 JOHN iii. 8.

THE BLESSING.

"O thou, my soul, do thou return
 Unto thy quiet rest,
For largely, lo, the Lord to thee
 His bounty hath exprest."

The Open Fountain.

"COME NOW, AND LET US REASON TOGETHER, SAITH THE LORD, THOUGH YOUR SINS BE AS SCARLET, THEY SHALL BE AS WHITE AS SNOW; THOUGH THEY BE RED LIKE CRIMSON, THEY SHALL BE AS WOOL." — *Isaiah* i. 18.

IF the judgments of God be a great deep, not less so are his mercies. The sinner may presume upon the one hand, or despair upon the other; but here is mercy made sure to the chief of sinners — here is glory to God, and yet joy to those who have rebelled against Him. Is conscience felt to be polluted? Is it like scarlet and like crimson, and is the sinner ready, like Job, to say, "Though I wash myself with snow-water, and make myself never so clean, yet mine own clothes will abhor me?" Even then the Holy One comes with the assurance that He will wash us, so that we shall be whiter than the snow. O my soul, thou knowest none so guilty as thyself — none so polluted and vile, for thou knowest none who have sinned against light, against privilege, against compassions like thine. Flee, then, to the much-needed fountain — there is safety, for there is purity, only there. And rejoice that the way is open — that the invitation is free. It is addressed to men whose sins are "as scarlet," or "red like crimson," and God is glorified when his mercy is welcomed. Welcome it, then, and live for evermore. But do not forget the divine alternative — "How shall we escape if we neglect the great salvation?" While all are welcome in the appointed way, yet "no man cometh to the Father but by the Son," and O, how soothing to the soul to walk in that path! It is "the way of peace." "The very God of peace" is our guide; "the covenant of peace" is our guarantee — a covenant as unchanging as the everlasting hills, while "the Prince of Peace" gladdens and sustains. Such honour have all his saints. My soul, in the sight of the heart-searching eye, is that honor thine?

But as God designed his people to be happy, far more is said of this peace — it is presented to us in the Word in many attractive forms. It is called "great peace;" it is described as "perfect peace;" it is spoken of as Christ's peace — nay, as the very "peace of God;" and can he be a loyal subject of the Prince of Peace who is still downcast and dejected?

THE PROOF.

"In that day there shall be a fountain opened to the house of David, and to the inhabitants of Jerusalem, for sin and for uncleanness." — ZECH. xiii. 1.

THE HYMN.

"All might" supplied — how gracious
  The God who spoke that word!
"All sin forgiven" — how precious
  Such mercy from our Lord!

"Complete in Christ" — Hosanna!
  The Judge will not disown;
Nay, "Ye are Christ's," and glory
  Awaits you on His throne.

The Almighty Advocate.

"WHEREFORE HE IS ABLE ALSO TO SAVE THEM TO THE UTTERMOST THAT COME UNTO GOD BY HIM, SEEING HE EVER LIVETH TO MAKE INTERCESSION FOR THEM." — *Heb.* vii. 25.

WILL he save a sinner such as I am? — a sinner against reason, against conscience, against providences, against experience, against the Word, against God — a sinner from my youth — a sinner in spite of vows the most solemn, and obligations the most binding? Is it possible that there can be hope for me? Even in Godhead, is there mercy to meet a case like mine?

Such are the questions sometimes asked by the earnest soul, when it is awakened from the delusions of sin, but has not yet discovered how God is glorified in pardoning. That soul can no longer make a mock at sin; nay, the arrows of the Almighty stick fast in the conscience, and no human hand can either extract them or heal the wound. When the Spirit arises in his might to "convince of sin, and righteousness, and judgment," the sinner is laid in the dust, and the evil heart of unbelief often suggests the question — "Is there pardon for *me?* for one so vile, so blinded, and perverse?"

The answer is — The High-Priest in the heavens can save to the uttermost all that come to God by him. That means, we must surpass the uttermost, and that means, we must accomplish an impossibility, before we can be beyond the reach of pardon, while we continue here below. The God and Father of our Lord Jesus Christ foreknew how suspicious and distrustful the awakened soul would be. Pledge upon pledge is therefore given, and all that can either encourage the downcast or rebuke the doubting, is recorded in the Word. The heavens are opened to our faith, as they were to Stephen's vision. We are permitted to behold the ever-living Intercessor there, pleading our cause, and making our peace secure. On the basis of his work finished on earth, he is prosecuting his high enterprise in the heavens. The earnest soul is thus interested in the intercession of one " whom the Father heareth always;" and when the God of truth announces that fact, should not every heart be faith, and every tongue be praise? " He can save unto the uttermost." " O, who is a God like unto thee, who passest by the transgression of the remnant of thy people?"

THE ASSURANCE.

"If any man sin, we have an Advocate with the Father, Jesus Christ the Righteous."—1 JOHN ii. 1.

THE HYMN.

"He who for men their surety stood,
 And poured on earth his precious blood,
 Pursues in heaven his mighty plan,
 The Saviour and the Friend of man."

Good Tidings of Great Joy.

"BEHOLD, I BRING YOU GOOD TIDINGS OF GREAT JOY, WHICH SHALL BE TO ALL PEOPLE."—*Luke* ii. 10.

A MESSAGE worthy of an angel's voice! A Saviour born — Omnipotence and helplessness combined — the Infinite and the finite in one — hope dawning on the despairing — happiness guaranteed to the wretched — peace with God made sure — the clouds and thick darkness which sin threw around Him cleared away — and the soul privileged once more to rejoice in the light of Jehovah's countenance — behold the substance of the heavenly message!

And these good tidings of great joy are "to all people." The desire of all nations has arrived. He has taken on Him the seed of Abraham. The day-star may now arise in men's hearts; and in every kindred, and nation, and tribe, and tongue, they may begin the anthem which is to be sung by the redeemed, world without end.

But are these good tidings for me? Yes, unless I refuse to receive them. May my soul listen to the heavenly message? It forsakes its own mercies if it refuse to welcome it. Would it not be presumption in me to seize upon the children's bread? The presumption lies in refusing what the Father offers. Hold out, then, the empty hand of faith;

stretch forth the withered arm; freely take what God so freely offers, and in taking it rejoice with a portion of the joy which is unspeakable. Does the sun shine freely on our homes? Do the breezes of heaven play without restraint around us, and does the fevered brow rejoice to feel their play? Is the dew gladdening to the tender plant? Is a mother's voice sweet to the child of her heart? Is the sight of his native land welcome to the exile and the outcast? or is its language a source of joy in a distant land? Surely not less joyous the glad tidings which the angel brought from heaven, when welcomed by the heart of man! These tidings embody all that even Jehovah could convey in the language of earth — pardon, peace, immortality, holiness, glory, God. These are the portion of the man that trembles at God's Word; and when all these are involved in one "unspeakable gift," who would not open the heart to welcome it?

THE PROOF.

"Why are ye fearful, O, ye of little faith?" — MATT. viii. 26.

THE CONVICTION.

"Though in the upward path to life
  The saint must often sigh,
Yet, trusting in our God, we find
  Delivering grace is nigh.

"When he who bade the world to be
  Has pledged his mighty power,
Bright hope may cheer the downcast soul, —
  No cloud need longer lower."

Love from God and to Him.

"GOD COMMENDETH HIS LOVE TOWARD US, IN THAT, WHILE WE WERE YET SINNERS, CHRIST DIED FOR US."—*Rom.* v. 8.

SUCH was the heart of man — so distrustful of God, so suspicious, and so estranged — that a mere announcement of the Father's love was not enough. Something was needed to attract attention to it — to demonstrate its depth — its ardor — its unquenchable nature. He accordingly commended it to us, and the mode of commending it was by the death of the Saviour *for sinners.* — Not for friends, but for enemies; not for loyal subjects, but for rebels; not for those who loved, but for creatures whose hearts were turned against their God — for these the Saviour died. Toward these the love of God in Christ was manifested, and the very hand that is lifted up in revolt may thus be gently taken down by the constraining love of Christ. That power which is paramount in heaven, becomes paramount on earth, at least in the heart of a believer; and a new moral principle, the love of the Redeemer to the lost, comes to reign in the bosom where enmity and rebellion reigned before.

O my soul, hast thou felt the power of that love, or art thou still a stranger to it? Hast thou cast away the weapons of thy rebellion, and art thou standing ready to exclaim, "Lord, thou knowest all things: thou knowest that I love thee?" Or art thou still indifferent, cold, unmoved, while God is commending his love to sinners, even the chief?

And O, how humbling is the discovery that the commendations with which God has surrounded his love are all in vain, unless the Holy Spirit unscale our eyes to see it, or melt our hearts to feel it! God is needed not merely to devise such a plan of redeeming love — or not merely to reveal it in our world: He is needed, moreover, to make us feel it; and never, never is the love of God in the gift of his Son felt or regarded at all, until the new-creating Spirit make all things new. O may that Spirit breathe on my soul, that it may live! His first fruit is love. May that appear in rich abundance in my soul — that He who is LOVE may be greatly glorified; and that I may never forget that the supreme proof of my love is to "keep his commandments."

THE PROOF.

"And we have known and believed the love that God hath to us. God is love; and he that dwelleth in love dwelleth in God, and God in him."—1 JOHN iv. 16.

THE HYMN.

"O Spirit, breathe that love divine,
Which fired the Saviour's soul,
Till linked in love to Him by Thee,
We own his blest control."

The Compassionate One.

"A BRUISED REED SHALL HE NOT BREAK; AND THE SMOKING FLAX SHALL HE NOT QUENCH."— *Isaiah* xlii. 3.

MAN heaps sin upon sin — God piles mercy upon mercy. It is a sport to man to do mischief — God waits to be gracious, and multiplies blessing upon blessing, even to the evil and the unthankful. Does he see a soul bowed to the earth with sorrow, mourning in its complaint, and making a noise, forsaken by father or mother, or, worst of all, weary and heavy laden with a burden of sin? Then that bruised reed he will not break. Nay, he will bind it up, and it is made whole, unless it thrust away the hand that would graciously heal. Or does he behold some soul like smoking flax — feeling after God — beginning to live for spiritual things — seeing men like trees walking, or just at the dawn of the day of small things? To that soul he gives strength, yea, he increases might, so that it becomes strong in the Lord. That heart which is love pities, that eye which never slumbers sees, that ear which is ever open to the cry of the feeble, hears the mourner's complaint. Strength is given according to his day; and at last he glories in tribulation, or blesses God because the heart has bled. O, who is a God like unto thee? and yet I have rebelled against thee! But though this be to my shame, I can only lean on the arm which I have impiously resisted; I can only cast myself on the mercy which I have despised; I can only try to lose my will in the will of him who doeth all things well. Prodigal as I am, I hasten to my Father's house. He will hear me, as he heard Ephraim bemoaning himself; and for him to hear is to pity. In those who seek him, he never saw a tear which he did not dry, nor witness a sorrow which he did not soothe. If the widow of Nain experienced his compassion, need I despair? If the helpless paralytic, after eight-and-thirty years of hope deferred, was made whole by his almighty word, should I question either his willingness or his power? Nay, I will take with me words, and return to Him from whom I have wandered — "I will arise and go to my father's house." "Return, then, to thy rest, O my soul." "O thou my soul, bless God the Lord."

THE PROOF.

"The LORD is gracious, and full of compassion; slow to anger, and of great mercy. The LORD is good to all; and his tender mercies are over all his works." — Ps. cxlv. 8, 9.

THE VOW.

"Thy grace shall dwell within my heart,
  And shed its fragrance there;
The noblest balm for all its wounds,
  The cordial of its care.

"The bruised One has borne our griefs,
  The Lamb of God our sins;
Then fear not — lo, the reign of love
  In ransomed souls begins."

Redemption Complete.

"IT IS FINISHED." — *John* xix. 30.

THE law of God is magnified and made honorable. Peace is now made between God and man, on terms which glorify the Holy One. The atonement is complete. Independent of man or man's power, the sure foundation is laid — an eye has been given for an eye, a tooth for a tooth, a hand for a hand, and a foot for a foot. Provision is made for cleansing the conscience. An end of transgression is made. An everlasting righteousness is brought in. The Holy Spirit is purchased and will be sent. A plea is provided for the chief of sinners, so that " *It is finished,*" spoken by the Saviour on the cross, may send a thrill of joy to the heart of the believing sinner upon earth, as it enhances the blessedness of the just made perfect in heaven.

"My soul is polluted," exclaims the humbled believer. " Pollution is finished by the blood which cleanses from it all," rejoins the Saviour on the cross, or from his throne in glory.

"The burden of my guilt is greater than I can bear," exclaims the self-condemned soul. " It is finished; there is no condemnation," is the reply of the Redeemer, as he waits to be gracious.

"I shall one day perish," is the expression of

the awakened conscience. "That is a thing impossible; a ransom has been found, and redemption is finished," is again the answer from the cross. Thy sins, though their name be legion, may all be swept away.

Freely take, then, what God has so freely provided, and be not faithless, but believing.

> ———————" When thoughts
> Of the last bitter hour come like a blight
> Over thy spirit, and sad images
> Of the stern agony, and shroud and pall,
> And breathless darkness, and the narrow house
> Make thee to shudder, and grow sick at heart,
> Go forth —"

— and looking in faith to the cross on which the Redeemer died as the substitute of his people, remember his last words and rejoice. The condemning power of sin is finished, and the prophecy of Daniel is fulfilled to every soul that believes.

THE PROOF.

"Seventy weeks are determined upon thy people, and upon thy holy city, to finish the transgression, and to make an end of sins, and to make reconciliation for iniquity, and to bring in everlasting righteousness, and to seal up the vision and prophecy, and to anoint the most Holy." — DANIEL ix. 24.

THE HYMN.

> "'Tis finished — The Messiah dies
>   For sins, but not his own;
> The great redemption is complete,
>   And Satan's power o'erthrown.
>
> "'Tis finished — all his groans are past,
>   His blood, his pain, and toils
> Have fully vanquished our foes,
>   And crowned him with their spoils."

Salvation Free.

"HO, EVERY ONE THAT THIRSTETH, COME YE TO THE WATERS, AND HE THAT HATH NO MONEY; COME YE, BUY, AND EAT; YEA, COME, BUY WINE AND MILK, WITHOUT MONEY AND WITHOUT PRICE." — *Isaiah* lv. 1.

WHY come? Because the invitation is addressed to sinners, and I am surely one. Am not I so athirst as to be weary and faint in my mind? Is not my soul like one that dwells in a dry parched land? Have I not felt that all this world can offer cannot satisfy my soul? I have fled to object after object, and listened to counsellor after counsellor. When one thing disappointed, I have tried another, and another; but all have failed. Rest seems to flee as I pursue it; and I can now only mourn in my complaint, and make a noise. If I say, Surely change of scene, or of friends, or pursuits, will bring relief, lo, vanity and vexation are stamped upon them, till I am compelled to say, "Miserable comforters are ye all." The delight of my eyes taken away with a stroke; my own familiar friend become my enemy; the object of my affection turned into bitterness; or to crown all, my sins pressing upon me like a load too heavy for me to bear and live; conscience accusing, the soul distempered and dismayed — surely these all urge me to flee to the fountain so full and so free!

But may I flee? One so guilty, one so perverse, or so far gone in sin — may *I* flee? To doubt it is to add sin to sin, to make God a liar, and therefore to render ruin sure. His language is, "Ho, every one that thirsteth, come." Away, then, unbelief — away all faltering and delay. When God invites, I will, through grace, comply. When God promises, I will, through grace, believe. When the Spirit and the Bride say, Come, I will go; and if I perish, I will perish in the arms of mercy, at the foot of the cross. But I should not be always laying the foundation of repentance from dead works. Nay, I should go on to perfection, and become strong in the Lord. For these purposes, I should live beside the throne of grace, for I am safe only when under its shadow, or linked to it by the golden chain of love. Come, then, O Breath, and breathe upon this soul, that it may open to the Saviour, like the little flower to the sunshine and the dew.

THE PROOF.

"He that hath received His testimony, hath set to his seal that God is true." — JOHN iii. 33.

THE RESOLUTION.

"Just as I am, though tossed about
With many a conflict, many a doubt,
Fightings within and fears without,
    O Lamb of God, I come."

The Righteousness of God.

"I BRING NEAR MY RIGHTEOUSNESS; IT SHALL NOT BE FAR OFF, AND MY SALVATION SHALL NOT TARRY: AND I WILL PLACE SALVATION IN ZION FOR ISRAEL MY GLORY." — *Isaiah* xlvi. 13.

HOW shall man be just with God? is the question which the awakened conscience clamors to have answered; and God himself answers it, saying, "I bring near my righteousness." Not the fallen creature's — that is tainted, and cannot justify. Not an angel's — he has none to spare. Not the righteousness of the just made perfect — "To which of the saints can we look?" But MINE. Jehovah our righteousness "shall not be far off."

Moreover, "My salvation shall not tarry." — Goaded by an accusing conscience, man may be urgent, impatient, and restless; he may wish to set a time to the Supreme, as if the creature would dictate instead of praying. But unmoved by all that, the Eternal conducts his kingdom according to his own wise and holy will, and meanwhile, of this the soul may be assured — salvation shall not tarry, that is, it will come at the set time; and when it comes, the soul will clearly see that that was the best time at once for the Holy One's glory, and the sinful one's humbling.

Farther, "I will place salvation in Zion for

Israel my glory." In the church the blessing shall be enjoyed, for that is the channel, as Jehovah is the fountain. "In the mount of the Lord's house it will be seen," and "I will glorify the house of my glory." Whether the sinner love them or no, the Lord loves the gates of Zion. There he meets with his people to gladden — there he unfolds his mind — there he explains the mysteries of providence, and the deeper mysteries of redemption. "Of Zion it shall be said, 'This man and that man was born in her,' and the Highest himself shall establish her." "All my springs are in thee."

Art thou, my soul, one of God's Israel, his glory? The Lord's portion is his people. Art thou of their number? Hath he made thee to differ — a vessel meet for the master's use — or for the inheritance of the saints in light? Then rejoice and be exceeding glad. Enter even here on the joy of your Lord, and let your life be a hymn to his praise.

THE PROOF.

"The kingdom of God is .... righteousness, and peace, and joy in the Holy Ghost." — ROM. xiv. 17.

THE RESOLUTION.

"No more, my God, I boast no more
   Of all the duties I have done;
I quit the hopes I held before,
   To plead the merits of thy Son.

"The best obedience of my hands
   Dare not appear before Thy throne;
But Jesus answered Thy demands —
   I plead, O Lord, what he hath done."

The Spirit of Jesus.

"NO MAN CAN SAY THAT JESUS IS THE LORD BUT BY THE HOLY GHOST."—1 *Cor.* xii. 3.

NO mother's affection, no father's authority, no pastor's teaching, can make me a believer in Jesus. He has no beauty that I should desire him, and his treatment from the Jews is his treatment from mankind, while we have only nature to teach us. But what shall I render to the Lord for all his benefits! The Spirit comes, and He takes of the things of Christ, and shows them to the soul. He unveils his beauty, by unscaling my eyes. He shows the Redeemer to be altogether lovely, and now like a child of Zion I bow to my Lord, and am joyful in my King. No more lip-homage and heart-rebellion. No more naming of his name only to dishonor it. No more walking in the footsteps of Judas, when he betrayed the Saviour with a kiss. I am one Spirit with the Lord. The Son now makes me free. Beholding his glory, the soul seeks to be transformed into his image. He becomes the very soul of the soul, its life, and being, and blessedness — its heaven while on the earth, and the heaven of its heaven on high. O my soul, has the Spirit taught thee to say that Jesus is thy Lord? Is he enthroned in the heart? Or is thy service mechanical, formal, and heartless still? An error here is fatal. To be right here is to be alive for evermore. And if the soul be indeed self-loving, it will seek to live in the Spirit, and to walk in the Spirit; to cultivate the fruits of the Spirit, and so to prepare for following the Lamb whithersoever he leadeth. The great promise of the Spirit is fulfilled to the New Testament church, as the great promise of the Saviour was, in the fulness of time, fulfilled to the Old. How strange, then, they who continue to grovel when they might soar — to sow to the flesh when they might sow to the Spirit! Into their assembly, mine honor, be not thou united! Nay, live by faith upon the Son of God. Let nothing tempt thee to pause till thou art personally and indissolubly united to the Lord, and made one spirit, one with him, "without which we are none of his."

THE PROOF.

"Hereby we know that he abideth in us, by the Spirit which he hath given us." — 1 JOHN iii. 24.

THE INVOCATION.

"Come, Holy Spirit, from above,
  Our longing breasts inspire
With the pure flame of heavenly love,
  And fan the sacred fire.

"We grieve Thee oft, and quench that flame
  Which lights the way to heaven,
But lead us in thy love to him
  In whom all is forgiven."

The Blood of Christ.

"IN THOSE DAYS, AND IN THAT TIME, SAITH THE LORD, THE INIQUITY OF ISRAEL SHALL BE SOUGHT FOR, AND THERE SHALL BE NONE; AND THE SINS OF JUDAH, AND THEY SHALL NOT BE FOUND: FOR I WILL PARDON THEM WHOM I RESERVE."— *Jer.* l. 20.

IT is sin that embitters life. It is the abominable thing which darkens our Father's countenance. It is sin that pollutes my conscience, and that mars my peace. It is sin that is the sting of death, and in the unpardoned that sting will cause the second death; it will be the cause of agony for ever.

And do I not feel that sin cleaves, in spite of me, to my soul? When I would do good, evil is present with me. It kneels down with me when I pray; it blends its offensive suggestions with my praise; it haunts me while I read the Word, or hear it; it intrudes alike amid the silence of the night, and the glare of day. Wherever self is sin will be found; in short, it haunts, and pollutes, and harasses the soul amid its very attempts to serve the Holy One.

But a voice is heard from heaven, and the Lord proclaims that "iniquity shall be sought for, and there shall be none," "and sins, but they shall not be found." They are cast into the depths of the sea. They are blotted out for ever. A sponge of extinction has passed over them, and the believer can now exult in the freedom which the Son of God bestows. He exclaims with David, "Blessed is he whose transgression is forgiven, whose sin is covered. Blessed is the man unto whom the Lord imputeth not iniquity, and in whose spirit there is no guile." Upon this subject the word of God has employed some of its strongest language. Here, if ever, line upon line is given to impress the mind alike with the freeness and the fulness of pardon. Till it be bestowed, man is in his best estate, a criminal already condemned, and hence the glad tidings of redemption through Christ's blood, even the forgiveness of sin; hence the duty of every soul that would not be self-deluded and self-destroyed, to press to an adjustment this simple but solemn question, Art thou pardoned? Glory to God in the highest, that the believer can be taught to exclaim, "I thank God for deliverance from the body of sin and death, through Jesus Christ my Lord," and "There is now no condemnation for them that are in Christ."

THE PROOF.

"The blood of Jesus Christ cleanses from all sin."
1 John i. 7.

THE HYMN.

"Glory to God on high!
  Let earth and skies reply,
  Praise ye his name!
His love and grace adore,
Who all our sorrows bore:
Sing aloud evermore,
    Worthy the Lamb."

The God of Pardons.

"I, EVEN I, AM HE THAT BLOTTETH OUT THY TRANSGRESSIONS FOR MINE OWN SAKE, AND WILL NOT REMEMBER THY SINS." — *Isaiah* xliii. 25.

"FOR MINE OWN SAKE" — that is the foundation of the Gospel, and the well-spring of hope to the sinner. All begins in grace, all is carried on by grace, and by grace the whole scheme of redemption is perfected. Man would fain find something in himself by which to move the unchanging One. My tears, my penitence, my suffering, my sacrifices, my faith, my religion: behold some of the considerations to which even the believer is prone to cling in the hope of influencing his God, or regaining his favor. But, "for mine own sake" — puts all these delusions aside. In the fathomless depths of the divine compassion; in that mercy which is like a great deep; in that grace which is to be measured, if measured at all, by the sufferings of the Son of God — in these alone do we find a foundation for hope. Man is utterly set aside. He is laid in the dust, and God alone is exalted to the throne. In no case will he, in no case *can* he, give his glory to another, and least of all when blotting out iniquity, and restoring the soul to purity again.

And mark, moreover, how this Almighty conde

scension speaks. "I, I am He ..... who will not remember thy sins." As if the Omniscient could forget! As if He who is the same yesterday, to-day, and for ever, could change! Now, when all this is said or done to re-assure the sinner, may he not boldly come for mercy to pardon? or if he still refuse under any pretext, may not the God of pardons renew the complaint—"What could have been done to my vineyard that I have not done in it?" O my soul, be it otherwise with thee! Commit thyself in well-doing to him who delights to pardon, and he will cause thee to delight "in the abundance of peace." "Put me in remembrance, let us plead together," are the gracious words of God. Plead, then, in faith, and God must change before thy hopes can fail.

THE INVITATION.

"Come, and let us join ourselves to the Lord in a perpetual covenant that shall not be forgotten."—JER. l. 5.

THE CONVICTION.

"Happy indeed the Christian's lot!
　His sins are all forgiven!
A gladdening hope beams o'er his soul,
　And points his heart to heaven.

"Worthy the Lamb, becomes his song;
　Who can condemn? he cries;
And while his life is hid with Christ,
　His heart is in the skies."

On Earth Peace.

"GLORY TO GOD IN THE HIGHEST, AND ON EARTH PEACE, GOOD-WILL TOWARD MEN."—*Luke* ii. 14.

MAN may forget his own chief end on earth — to glorify his God — but the heavenly host never forget the purpose of their being. They praised their God when his word gave the world birth. They praised Him when the Saviour came to do their work on earth. Another joy is felt by them — and another, and another — as soul after soul repents; and "Glory to God in the highest," is ever the burden of their hosanna.

And O, what a topic! glory to God and peace to man in unison! Glory to God in man's death had not been strange, for it is right and reasonable that sin should suffer. But peace on earth, at the price of the blood of Him who was Jehovah's fellow — peace on earth purchased by the agonies and the death of the Lamb of God — good-will toward men made sure by the sufferings of an almighty Substitute — that was the most amazing topic — the most entrancing song of the angels.

And hast thou learned, my soul, at least to lisp it? On earth there is peace. The Prince of Peace bestows it. Dost thou enjoy it? There is "good-will toward men." Dost thou believe it? or is God still viewed as a hard taskmaster, giving with reluctance, and delighting rather to withhold? It is just at this point that the evil heart of unbelief is often unmasked; here even the believer is made painfully aware that the great controversy which began when Adam believed the tempter and denied the word of his God, is not yet adjusted. Most of our misery here below may be traced up to the evil heart of unbelief as its fountain, and happy they to whom it is given to believe; in whom faith works by love, and purifies the heart, and overcomes the world, because it receives and rests upon Christ.

And to urge the soul forward in that direction, meditate on what it is to doubt the Word of the Eternal. It is to imitate the tempter — to make God a liar — not merely to place a creature beside him, but to lift that creature into the throne! Surely the soul should recoil with horror from such impiety; and yet that is habitually done by the evil heart of unbelief.

THE PROOF.

"As I live, saith the Lord God, I have no pleasure in the death of the wicked; but that the wicked turn from his way and live: turn ye, turn ye, from your evil ways; for why will ye die, O house of Israel?" — EZEK. xxxiii. 11.

THE PRAYER.

"Grant, O my God, this one request:
O be thy love alone
My ample portion — here I rest,
For heaven is in the boon."

D*

The Glorious Gospel.

"IN DUE TIME CHRIST DIED FOR THE UNGODLY."—*Rom.* v. 6.

NOT for the virtuous: In God's eye there are none such, for all "are become filthy." Not for the penitent: For "Christ is exalted a Prince and a Saviour to grant repentance," and none can possess it till they come to Christ to obtain it. Not for the reformed: For in God's estimation there is no valid reformation till men be in Christ, and become new creatures under the converting power of the Spirit. Not even for believers: For "faith is itself a gift of God," and cannot be the procuring cause of his favor.

"For the ungodly" then: For sinners, even the chief—for those who are by nature the children of wrath, or dead in trespasses and in sin—for these did the Redeemer die; and this is the glorious gospel of the grace of God—Salvation for the chief of sinners. Man would be satisfied were he permitted to think that his tears at least, or his sighs, and his contrition, had some share in procuring the favor of his God; but that is only a portion of "the smoke from the abyss." The sighs, and tears, and contrition of a sinner are all tainted by sin, and they can, therefore, obtain from God only condemnation. In his wisdom and compassion, then, these are the terms of the Gospel: "When we were without strength, in due time Christ died for the ungodly"— for those who were without God in the world, who were aliens from hope, and who had in themselves no portion but sin, no heritage but despair. And this is the sheet anchor of the self-condemned. Here is the divine method of meeting the law's demands, of satisfying the challenges of conscience, and teaching us to join in the noble anthem, "Who shall lay any thing to the charge of God's elect?" Rejoice, then, and be exceeding glad, O my soul, for here are the good news — Christ died for the ungodly. Hold up the hands which hang down, for Christ died for sinners, even the chief — for the ungodly to make them godly — for sinners to make them saints.

THE PROOF.

"Christ gave himself for us, that he might redeem us from all iniquity, and purify unto himself a peculiar people, zealous of good works." — TITUS ii. 14.

THE REJOICING.

"Not to the terrors of the Lord,
The tempest, fire, and smoke;
Not to the thunder of that word
Which God on Sinai spoke —

"But we are come to Zion's hill,
The city of our God,
Where milder words declare his will,
And spread his love abroad."

Grace Abounding.

"GO YE INTO ALL THE WORLD, AND PREACH THE GOSPEL TO EVERY CREATURE."—*Mark* xvi. 15.

WHO would limit the good news from God to man? Who would circumscribe the outflowing of divine love? Who would monopolize the antidote to misery? Who would fence round the fountain open for sin? Barbarian, Scythian, bond and free, all need the healing power; and let them enjoy it freely as the wind or the sunlight of heaven. Man may fetter what Jehovah makes free. Man may limit to a caste, a tribe, a sect, what the only wise God commanded to be spread wherever there are sinners to be saved, or sorrows to be soothed; but that is because man is prone to oppose the mandate of his God. Come, then, my soul, and freely rejoice in what thy God so freely offers. Beware, lest thou place limits where God places none; in that thou wilt only mar thy peace, by marring God's Gospel. True, many are called, while few find the narrow way; but that is because men will not come to Christ, that they may have life. Come, then, to the fountain, and there rejoice in the loving-kindness of the Lord. And while you draw nigh, be encouraged by the thought that as the Saviour was condemned in the believer's behalf, they that believe need fear no evil—the Holy One cannot condemn both the sinner and the substitute. He cannot exact payment of the same debt twice; and that is the impregnable principle on which the hopes of the believer repose. Every form of human religion is founded on some fiction — Romanism, Islamism, Hinduism — all that man has invented is built upon something in man — his sufferings, his righteousness, his prayers. The Saviour alone has based his religion upon the justice of God, and there the soul is safe, for the very holiness and truth of Jehovah are now upon its side. And upon our side for what? Perhaps to allure man into the wilderness; but why? Is it to destroy him, as natural conscience is prone to suggest? Nay, it is to speak words to our heart — to give us vineyards from the very wilderness, and make even the valley of Achor a door of hope.

THE PROOF.

" The hope of the gospel, ... was preached to every creature which is under heaven." — Col. i. 23.

THE HYMN.

" Great God! the treasures of thy love
    Are everlasting mines:
Deep as our boundless miseries,
    And countless as our sins.

" The world were sunless if that love
    Were not in Christ revealed;
But when in him we own thy power,
    Thou art a sun and shield."

The Almighty Promiser.

"FOR THE MOUNTAINS SHALL DEPART, AND THE HILLS BE REMOVED; BUT MY KINDNESS SHALL NOT DEPART FROM THEE, NEITHER SHALL THE COVENANT OF MY PEACE BE REMOVED, SAITH THE LORD THAT HATH MERCY ON THEE." — *Isaiah* liv. 10.

THE very word which commanded the world to be, is the foundation of a sinner's hope. He who hung the earth upon nothing — who weighs the hills in scales, and the mountains in a balance — who can measure the ocean in the hollow of his hand, or take up the isles as a very little thing — has spoken the word, and on that word the believer reposes. That is his munition of rocks: he dwells in safety there beyond the reach of woe. Jehovah must change, ere the believer be cast off.

And hear how the Almighty Promiser gives assurance upon assurance that the believer is thus safe. What so stable as the mountains? what so abiding as the hills? Yet these are transient and shadowy things, compared with the foundation of a sinner's hope — they may pass away, but the word of the Lord endureth for ever. The kindness of God is thus guaranteed by line upon line. It is a covenant of peace which he has made; and when we take hold of that, joy is sown for the righteous, and gladness for the upright in heart. The Lord God is a sun and shield, he will give grace and glory; yea, "The Lord is my rock, and my fortress, and my deliverer;

my God, my strength, in whom I will trust; my buckler, the horn of my salvation, and my high tower." What, then, need disturb that soul's serenity, or what can endanger its safety? Is it not more than a conqueror, through him that loved us? Could we learn the lesson of resting simply on the truth of God, unshaken by trials, unmoved by providences, and confiding exclusively in *grace*, the very God of Peace would see his image reflected from our souls again. He would dwell in us, and walk in us, and rank us among his sons and daughters. He might lead us through trial after trial, and the dark valley at the last must be assuredly trod. But if He be there — and we have the assurance that he is with the believing soul — what evil need we fear, or what enemy need trouble us?

THE PROOF.

"Thou wilt keep him in perfect peace, whose mind is stayed on thee: because he trusteth in thee." — ISAIAH xxvi. 3.

THE HYMN.

"Firm as his throne his covenant stands,
    Though earth and sky depart;
No change, no want, no woe to those
    Graved on the Saviour's heart.

"I long for peace, and Christ is that:
    For hope — its radiance beams
In him in whom the Father's love
    On drooping mortals gleams."

The Way to the Father.

"NO MAN COMETH TO THE FATHER BUT BY ME."—*John* xiv. 6.

I CAN draw near by the blood of calves and of goats, exclaimed the Jew, who could not penetrate further than the letter of his religion. I can draw near with a mangled and mutilated body, exclaims the Hindu, gasping out his life in the frantic attempt to appease his bloody god. I can approach in the strength of an incantation, or by means of my fetish, rejoins the embruted African. My penance, my fasting, my self-inflicted anguish, will open the way for me, re-echoes the deluded Romanist. My sound creed will throw open a path for me into the presence of God, is the whisper of the formalist, or the man who thinks there can be religion without conversion, or salvation without a new heart. But he who has the key of David, who opens and no man shuts, and shuts and no man opens, comes among these deluded ones and says, "I am the way, the truth, and the life; no man cometh to the Father but by me."

It is *exclusive*. There is absolutely none other. Even to attempt to find another is sin; it is dishonoring to the Son of God.

It is a *blood-marked* way. For it was opened through the rent vail of a Mediator's flesh.

It is a *living* way. The dead cannot walk there.

The first step in it is taken when the life-giving Spirit turns our feet into the way of peace.

It is a *little-frequented* way. "Few there be that find it." The invitation is free to all; but as men must drop the love of sin when they enter on that path, it is shunned by countless myriads. Yet it is a way in which men walk with God — a way which leads to something better than the city of refuge, even the city of our God. It is a path in which our companions are all they that fear Him, or have turned their faces Zionward, and in which the Spirit of God is our guide. He is like a voice behind us saying, "This is the way, walk ye in it."

And such being the way, am I walking there? "It shall be called the way of holiness; the unclean shall not pass over it;" and is that verified in me? Have I brought my sins into the holy path, or did I through grace forsake them at the entrance?

THE PROOF.

"And an highway shall be there, and a way, and it shall be called The way of holiness; the unclean shall not pass over it." — ISAIAH xxxv. 8.

THE RESOLUTION.

"O Lord, in the strength thou has given,
Or pledged thy sure word to bestow,
I will climb the steep pathway to heaven,
And exult in thy grace as I go."

Look and Live.

"LOOK UNTO ME AND BE YE SAVED, ALL THE ENDS OF THE EARTH: FOR I AM GOD, AND THERE IS NONE ELSE."—*Isaiah* xlv. 22.

HAD it been said, Torture yourselves and be saved, all would have understood, and many would have obeyed. Or had it been said, Give the fruit of thy body for the sin of thy soul, that also would have been plain, and, revolting as it is, many would have hastened to present the offering. Or had it been said, Go on some weary pilgrimage, compass sea and land, climb rugged ascents upon your bare and bended knees, and be saved; all would again have understood the saying. Self-righteousness would have been gratified, and then at all hazards, men would have complied.

But merely to "look and be saved," is what man cannot comprehend. "Heaven's easy, artless plan," of suspending eternal life, and the favor of God, on a thing so simple, or so unearthly, transcends the wisdom of man, and the difficulty is increased when it is said, "Look, ye blind," as if salvation involved at once impossibilities and contradictions.

But, O my soul, let us exalt God's name together, because our salvation is so easy and so simple. "Look and live." "Come unto me and live." "Believe and live"—behold the first principle of the Christian faith—a principle which, like the first link in a perfect chain, draws all the others after it. Rejoice that it is not some mighty sacrifice, but simply a look of faith, that God our Saviour asks; and then looking to him as our "God, besides whom there is none else," you may delight in the abundance of peace.

And do not say, "I cannot look;" as if God were mocking us when he invites us to draw nigh. Do not plead inability; as if God did not know, or did not pity our helplessness. Surely you can come, or you can look, *as a sinner!* Surely you can cast yourself upon His mercy as one of *the ungodly.* That is your character, as God describes it. To you, in that character, is this salvation sent. Away, then, with all doubts, all delays and hesitation, that the soul may at once be saved and blessed.

THE PROOF.

"Come unto me, all ye that labor and are heavy laden, and I will give you rest."—MATT. xi. 28.

THE COUNSEL.

"Behold, my soul, with beaming eye,
    The throne where thy Redeemer **stands,**
Thy glorious Advocate on high,
    With costly incense in his hands.

"All, all is free as air to thee,
    Just look and be forgiven;
Then pardon, peace, 'the peace of **God,**'
    Shall shed the light of heaven."

The Abundance of Peace.

"THOU HAST ASCENDED ON HIGH, THOU HAST LED CAPTIVITY CAPTIVE: THOU HAST RECEIVED GIFTS FOR MEN; YEA, FOR THE REBELLIOUS ALSO, THAT THE LORD GOD MIGHT DWELL AMONG THEM." — *Psalm* lxviii. 18.

NO man can be truly happy but the believer in Jesus; for surely no man can be happy while he lies under the load of unpardoned sin, and therefore under the wrath of the Holy One.

But when sin is pardoned, and God our friend, how jubilant may the soul become — how full, how perfect is its peace; how rich its portion, how exhaustless its joy! Light is now sown for the righteous, and gladness for the upright in heart. The Prince of Peace is at once that soul's Saviour and its portion. It may walk with "the very God of peace." It may enjoy "the peace of God which passeth all understanding;" or to say all in one, "the kingdom of God is within it;" and that is "righteousness, and peace, and joy in the Holy Ghost." He who led captivity captive, and received gifts for men, even for the rebellious, has taught them to walk with God again. The Lord God is to dwell in them, and walk in them. He is to be their God, and they are to be his sons and daughters.

But the GIFTS which the Prince of Peace thus received for men are countless. Does the believer veer and change? The unchanging one is now his portion. Does he sin? The God of pardons blots out iniquity. Does the believer pray? God hears and answers. Is the believer afraid? His God defends. Is he bereaved and sad? His God comforts. Is the believer poor? He who led captivity captive imparts unsearchable riches. In short, his God is a little sanctuary to him. He hides the believer in the hollow of his hand, and even his dying chamber may be turned into the ante-room of glory. Why, then, should the believer in Jesus be downcast and gloomy? Why should he hang down his head like a bulrush? Why act as if his God were not the Prince of Peace? Away, my soul, with that evil report against the truth. The Lord will no more forget his people, than a mother will forget the infant of her love. Arise, then, from the dust. Look up to the Sun of Righteousness. Reflect some rays of his brightness; walk like a child of the light, and so win others to walk with thee.

THE PROOF.

"Can a woman forget her sucking child, that she should not have compassion on the son of her womb? yea, they may forget, yet will I not forget thee." — ISAIAH xlix. 15.

THE HYMN.

" As countless as the midnight stars
Bright as the mid-day sun,
And sure as is Jehovah's oath,
Are the joys our Captain won."

The Price of Redemption.

"RETURN UNTO ME, FOR I HAVE REDEEMED THEE."—*Isaiah* xliv. 22.

SUCH is the gracious invitation of God to his wandering people. On the right hand and on the left they forsake his ways. The veriest trifle succeeds in enticing them away from him. Upon every high mountain, and under every green tree, they sin against their God. But though they forget him, his affections are still set on them — he commands them, nay, He entreats them to return. His compassion is moved at their self-destruction, and by mercy upon mercy he would regain their confidence and their heart. And O, mark, my soul, the ground on which God rests his plea — " Return . . . . . for I have redeemed thee." Not creation — that had long ago failed to bind the creature to the Creator. Not providence — that also was unavailing, for man snatched at the gift, and neglected the Giver. But Redemption — that supplied the motives which were destined to win back man's wayward heart, or to prove that it could not be won. The precious blood of Christ, as the price of redemption; his agonies, and tears, and death, as the means of working it out; his love, which many waters could not quench, nor universal enmity subdue; these are the moral powers appointed to sway man's soul; and swayed by these, the soul should return to its God to rejoice in the liberty which the Son bestows.

But has my heart yielded to that appeal, or am I still stout-hearted and far from righteousness? Am I redeemed by the precious blood of Christ, or do I rather trample upon the blood of the covenant, and count it an unholy thing? Blessed are they who listen to that appeal! They shall be still praising God. Who is he that shall harm them? Of them Jehovah has said, "This people have I formed for myself, they shall show forth my praise." The longer that I strive to "work out my own salvation," according to the Word of God, I feel the more need to make sure that that salvation is *personal*—that it is "my own." May the Spirit of all grace teach me to say, as the Word of God warrants—"The Lord is my shepherd," and "Christ loved me, and gave himself for me."

THE PROOF.

"Forasmuch as ye know that ye were not redeemed with corruptible things, as silver and gold, from your vain conversation received by tradition from your fathers; but with the precious blood of Christ, as of a lamb without blemish and without spot."— 1 Pet. i. 18, 19.

THE COUNSEL.

"Wretched, ruined, helpless soul,
To a Saviour's blood apply,
He alone can make thee whole;
Fly to Jesus, sinner, fly."

Gold Tried in the Fire.

"I COUNSEL THEE TO BUY OF ME GOLD TRIED IN THE FIRE."—*Rev.* iii. 18.

IT is the delusive thought of all men by nature as well as of the lukewarm Laodiceans, that they are rich, and increased in goods, and in need of nothing. They are proud of their very rags, and would offer to God, as a price for his favor, the very thing which he declares that he hates. But the God of the gospel offers the unsearchable riches — the incorruptible inheritance — the crown of glory which fadeth not away. It is true, we read, "I counsel thee to buy," but no less true that it is "without money and without price." All is a gift — a free gift — an unspeakable gift from God to man. There is rest to the weary. There is peace to the troubled. There is health to the diseased. There is hope for the despairing. There is life for the dead; and O, my soul, is not that as refreshing to the soul as Elim and its palm trees to the wanderers in the desert? Have we not here vineyards from the wilderness? May we not dig up wells in this valley of Baca, or pluck leaves from the tree which is for the healing of the nations? There is no want to them that fear God. They have gold tried in the fire, and far more than all the gold of Ophir could buy.

The eye rejoices to wander over the green earth,

and remember that it is the Lord's, and the fulness thereof. It delights to gaze upon the midnight sky, and meditate on the wonders which are there beheld — the mighty, silent procession of all those innumerable orbs. It looks upon the sea sleeping in its beauty, or swelling in its mightiness — now the emblem of Him who is love — and now of Him who will " by no means clear." But none of these things, neither earth, nor sky, nor ocean, can tell us aught of *grace*, of *pardon*, or of *mercy*. They utter no voice in reply to the question " How shall man be just before his God?" For an answer to that, we must apply to the cross, and blessed are they who have ears to hear, and a heart to understand its language.

THE PROOF.

"Thanks be unto God for his unspeakable gift." — 2 Cor. ix. 15

THE INVITATION.

" Come all ye pining, hungry poor,
　The Saviour's bounty taste;
Behold a never-failing store,
　For every aching breast.

" No price is asked — none ye can bring
　Free like the air of heaven,
And gentle as the evening dew,
　Grace bids you be forgiven."

Grace and Glory.

"HE SHALL BRING FORTH THE HEADSTONE WITH SHOUTINGS OF GRACE, GRACE UNTO IT." — *Zech.* iv. 7.

GRACE — or the free favor of God — lays the foundation of hope to man. Grace rears the structure, and watches over it at every stage of its progress. Were it not so, it would speedily crumble, like some of the structures reared by man, into premature decay. And when the fabric shall be completed — when the copestone has been put on, and all made perfect and complete according to the will of God, the acclamation will still be — Grace! grace! The wise Master-Builder thus presides over the whole spiritual temple; and the beauty of holiness is in consequence the ornament which signalizes the structure.

The sure foundation laid in Zion, then, is laid by grace. All who build on it are guided by grace; and when the house not made with hands becomes the home of the ransomed, grace will admit us there, and hand us over to glory.

Now, art thou, my soul, in preparation for that dwelling-place of glory? Hast thou been rescued by grace from the grasp of sin? Are thy hopes built on the exclusive foundation — that which God has laid — "that rock which is Christ?" Then rejoice in the Lord alway; and again, I say rejoice.

To his people he will speak peace, but let them not return again to foolishness. Clothed in his own righteousness, and upheld by his right arm, they need not fear though ten thousand were set round about against them. The Lord will help, and that right early.

Right early: — not to-morrow — before to-morrow I may be laid out for the grave. Not after I have repented — before I can repent, I must come to Him who grants repentance. Not after I have reformed what is wrong, and rectified what God condemns in my conduct. That reformation will never be effectual; it will reach only to the hand, and never touch the heart, until I return to my God as he invites. *Right early,* then — now and without one hour's delay, I will wait on God, that He may renew my strength.

THE PROOF.

"By grace ye are saved." — Eph. ii. 5.

THE HYMN.

Thy grace my wayward heart first won;
  Thy grace still holds me fast;
Thy grace completes the work begun,
  And guides me home at last.

"How baseless are our dreams of worth
  While godless all our ways!
O, can pollution proudly meet,
  The Judge's flame-bright gaze?"

The Gift of God.

"THE GIFT OF GOD IS ETERNAL LIFE THROUGH JESUS CHRIST OUR LORD."— *Romans* vi. 23.

HOW earnest is the God of the Bible that sinners should be assured that all we enjoy is a gift from Him! Man is constantly claiming; God as constantly sets that claim aside, and offers all as a gift. Is it received? Then God is glorified, and self-ruined man is laid in the dust. Eternal life is a gift. Faith is a gift. The Holy Spirit is a gift. The Saviour is God's unspeakable gift. The privilege of suffering for His sake is a gift. Mercy is a gift. Peace is a gift. Pardon at last, as well as all that fits us to enjoy it, is a gift; and, by the constant repetition of that truth, the pride of the self-righteous soul is reproved; the claims of men for God's favor are disowned: they must submit to be saved by grace, or never saved at all.

Now, when the soul clearly discerns that truth, it begins, for the first time, to be happy. As long as the idea of merit, or deserving the favor of God, haunts the soul, it is wretched, and harassed by legal fear. It never can be sure that it has done enough, or repented enough, or suffered enough. But when the gift of God is received — when man perceives that the only thing he can deserve, or the only wages he can earn, is death — pride is hidden from him, and he begins to rejoice in the unspeakable gift. Rejoice then, O my soul, that eternal life is to be obtained for the taking. God offers: Dost thou welcome? Christ has purchased — grace bestows: Art thou waiting to receive? Then go in peace, thy faith has made thee whole. The second death has no more power over thee; the original curse is repealed — or rather, it is exhausted by the Saviour for thee; and thy blessedness, now and for ever, should be, to rejoice in Christ Jesus, and have no confidence in self.

How strange were the world to continue in darkness after the sun has risen! How strange were the earth to continue congealed, and the forests leafless, after the genial suns of spring and summer bid them put on their beauty! And can it be less strange for the soul, visited, redeemed, and saved by the Son of God, to walk only in sackcloth — in the gloom of Sinai, not the sunshine of Zion!

THE PROOF.

"My peace I *give* unto you: not as the world giveth, give I unto you." — JOHN xiv. 27.

THE ASSURANCE.

"Poor sinful, thirsty, fainting souls,
Are freely welcome here;
Salvation, like a river, rolls
Abundant, broad, and clear."

The Refuge of Lies.

"WE HAVE MADE LIES OUR REFUGE, AND UNDER FALSEHOOD HAVE WE HID OURSELVES."— *Isaiah* xxviii. 15.

IS it not a lie to think that we can resist Omnipotence, and prosper? Is it not a lie to suppose that we can rush upon the bosses of Jehovah's buckler, and escape unscathed? Is it not a lie, to act as if what the Holy One pronounces to be "filthy rags" could suffice for a protection in the day when he arises to judgment? Is it not a lie, to think that the creature can satisfy the soul, though we feel that it melts away while we try to grasp it? Is it not a lie, to suppose that sin can afford pleasure to the soul, while it draws down the wrath of God, and ripens us for everlasting burnings? Yet these, and such as these, are the delusions to which men cling: to these they flee, in the hope that they can find a refuge there from Him whose eyes are as a flame of fire. A converted Chinese once said that he might as well seek shelter from a thunderbolt behind his own shadow, as from the justice of God behind his own righteousness; and will not that man rise up in judgment against those who seek an asylum in lies?

But bless the Lord, O my soul! He who is the Truth has been here. He came to withdraw us from our refuges of lies, by showing how they crumble above us, and threaten to bury us in their ruins. He answered the question, What is truth? by the announcement, "I am the Truth;" the truth concerning God — the truth concerning man — and the truth concerning the mode of making them walk together like those who are agreed. Hast thou then, O my soul, learned that truth, and has it made thee free? Are the devices of the evil heart, and of the father of lies, now an abomination to thee? Then the Spirit of truth has led thee to the God of truth. No refuge of lies will satisfy thee. The Rock that is higher than we will be thy confidence, and "a man shall be a hiding-place from the wind, and a covert from the tempest, like rivers of water in a dry place, and the shadow of a great rock in a weary land."

THE PROOF.

"When he, the Spirit of truth, is come, he will guide you into all truth." — JOHN xvi. 13.

THE HYMN.

"Enamored of lies, see the victim of sin
  Rush on through delusion to death;
But Jesus, 'THE TRUTH,' tears these refuges down,
  To shed heaven's light on our path."

Faith.

"THE JUST SHALL LIVE BY FAITH."—*Romans* i. 17.

How mighty, yet how weak, is faith! How mysterious, yet how simple! How prized in the religion of God! How undervalued or perverted in that of man!

What is its province? What is the secret of its power? Has it any inherent virtue? How does it save? How does it sanctify? How does it overcome the world? What secret spell does faith possess, when all these things are ascribed to it? The one answer to all these questions is, that *faith receives Christ;* and hence all its power. In itself it is nothing — it can do nothing; but when it welcomes or embraces the Lord, then it can do all things. It can lead to the fountain opened for sin. It can purify the heart. It can overcome the world. With the Spirit of God for its Author — with the Word of God for its foundation — with Christ for the great object to which it clings — with the salvation of the soul for its end — faith leads us in triumph along the narrow way. It is the evidence of things not seen. It is the substance of things hoped for. It puts on the Saviour's righteousness, and is safe. It teaches the soul in trial to say, "Though he slay me, yet will I trust in Him." It points, amid danger, to Him who is our hiding-place from the storm, and it tells, in the day of prosperity, of the Sun of Righteousness. In a word, faith receives and rests on Christ. Hence its more than mortal power; hence its triumphs; hence it has led many to the stake amid songs of joy. Or, far more than that, hence it obtains from God, as an empty hand held out obtains an alms, the righteousness which justifies — the blood which cleanses — the peace which is the foretaste of heaven. The language of faith is, "I can do all things through Christ which strengtheneth me" — "I will not fear though ten thousand be set round about against me" — "The name of the Lord is a strong tower." I flee thither and am safe, and if my faith "work by love," all is well — "All things are possible; only believe" — "Lord, I believe; help thou mine unbelief" — "Lord, increase our faith" — Should not these be the cherished sentiments of every self-loving soul?

THE PROOF.

"Now faith is the substance of things hoped for, the evidence of things not seen." — HEB. xi. 1.

THE HYMN.

"Faith clings to an Almighty arm,
Faith pleads Almighty grace;
And resting there, rejoices
In God our Righteousness."

Jehovah our Righteousness.

"THE LORD OUR RIGHTEOUSNESS."—*Jer.* xxiii. 6.

TO this name of the Lord faith rejoices to cling, as the ivy clings to the wall, or the vine-tree to the prop which sustains it. "Wherewithal shall we appear before God?" is the question which the soul begins to agitate as soon as the Spirit makes it alive to eternal realities; and, in agitating that question, it finds no solid resting-place until it can present something perfect to the eye of the Judge. But where shall that be found? The earth says, It is not in me; the deep proclaims, It is not in me. It cannot be gotten for silver, nor purchased for gold. But when all else fails; or, when "miserable comforters are ye all," is found written on all that is mortal, THE LORD OUR RIGHTEOUSNESS is revealed; and to Him faith clings, as the drowning cling to the cable which is thrown to save them. We are made the righteousness of God in Him, while He is made sin for us; and by that blessed exchange, the sinner is restored to the favor of God. For justification, he is complete in Christ — he is accepted in the beloved; and proceeds in the path of personal holiness, to prepare to be presented unto God without spot or wrinkle, or any such thing.

But why are we debarred from pleading **our**

own righteousness? Because it is polluted. And why are we invited to make mention of Christ's righteousness, even of it only? Because it only is perfect and complete. God cannot refuse to justify us through it, *because it is His own;* and therefore, clothed in that, the believer stands in the presence of the Heart-searcher rejoicing in Christ Jesus, and praising God for a complete salvation.

Is it the case then, O my soul, that *thou* canst plead the righteousness of Christ? Is that the rock of thy salvation — the foundation of thy hope — in the prospect of meeting God? Then the Spirit, the glorifier of Jesus, is thy Teacher; and thy language may humbly be, "Who shall lay any thing to the charge of God's elect? It is God that justifies; who is he that condemns? It is Christ that died, yea rather, that is risen again:" and "he died for our sins, and rose for our justification."

THE PROOF.

"For he hath made him to be sin for us, who knew no sin that we might be made the righteousness of God in him." — 2 Cor. v. 21.

THE PLEA.

"I plead the merits of the Son,
  Who died for sinners on the tree;
I plead His righteousness alone —
  O put the spotless robe on me."

The New Heart.

"MARVEL NOT THAT I SAID UNTO THEE, YE MUST BE BORN AGAIN."—*John* iii. 7.

MARVEL at it no more than to be told that the birds of the air cannot live in the depths of the ocean, nor the fishes of the deep in the blue sky above us. Man was created to work for God's eternal favor, and win it: he must have a new nature before he will simply believe for it. Man was created at first for the love of God: he is now enmity against him; and must have a new nature ere he can love Him again. Man was created for the service of God, and found his delight therein: that service is now a weariness to him; and new likings must be created ere he can delight in God's service any more. Hence the Saviour's word, "Ye must be born again;" hence the assurance, that "unless we be converted, and become like little children, we cannot see the kingdom of God;" and hence the intimation, that "if any man be in Christ, he is a new creature; old things have passed away, and all things have become new."

Now, is it true, my soul, that this all-decisive change has come over thee? Hast thou felt and submitted to the Spirit's new creative energy? If thou canst not name the day, or the occasion when that took place, art thou sure of *the fact?* Art thou practising no deception on thyself? Art thou honestly willing to know the truth of thy condition? And hast thou reason to be assured that thou art indeed alive unto God? Then walk in the Spirit, and cherish the things of the Spirit. As thou hast borne the image of the first Adam, see that thou bear the image of the second. Being born of God, O live like the child of a king, and the heir of a kingdom, and thus be blessed in thy deeds.

But O how prone men are to be self-satisfied! Though the Saviour has placed the great truth of regeneration or conversion on the very frontier of his kingdom, and said, with the deepest emphasis that words can convey, that there is no other mode of ingress, many think that they are in the kingdom, while yet they never thought of conversion; they either ignore, or pervert, or deny regeneration. But blessed are all they who are born of the Spirit, or born of God through the incorruptible seed. They who are so shall never be moved.

THE PROOF.

"And I will put my spirit within you, and cause you to walk in my statutes, and ye shall keep my judgments, and do them."— EZEK. xxxvi. 27.

THE HYMN.

"The new-creating Spirit's power
Dispels the reign of death,
And guides the soul that knew not **God**
Along the heavenward path."

Godly Sorrow.

"THEY SHALL LOOK UPON ME WHOM THEY HAVE PIERCED, AND THEY SHALL MOURN FOR HIM AS ONE MOURNETH FOR HIS ONLY SON, AND SHALL BE IN BITTERNESS FOR HIM, AS ONE THAT IS IN BITTERNESS FOR HIS FIRSTBORN." — *Zech.* xii. 10.

COUNTLESS crowds never do so. Far from feeling the poignant sorrow which the Holy Spirit here describes, sin occasions no regret, and the Saviour's anguish no lamentation. Nay, men are busy piercing him afresh, as far as they have the power. His love unto death is unheeded. His compassion for the lost and the wretched awakens no corresponding emotion. Men are in spirit ready to cry as of old, "Away with him; crucify him, crucify him."

But not so all. The Spirit of grace and of supplications is poured out on some. They then discover what it is to have been sharers in the guilt of crucifying the Saviour, and of adding to the poignancy of his dying agonies. They now understand the strong language of the Spirit: "They shall be in bitterness for him as one is in bitterness for his firstborn," and feel that the dust is their becoming bed, or sackcloth their becoming garment.

O my soul, there is an eye upon thee which looks thee through and through. Conscience may be quick, but the glance of that eye is keener still.

It discovers whether thou hast ever mourned for a Saviour's agony, or whether thou art still as wayward as ever. How, then, is it with thee? Hast thou felt what it is to be a sinner? Hast thou seen the enormity of sin as committed against Him whose love was boundless, and reached even to thee? Then rejoice that some even of his crucifiers were washed in the blood which they helped to shed, when an apostle preached salvation to them through Him whom they had crucified and slain. Away with all thy sins to Him. Look on Him whom thou hast pierced; and then, with godly sorrow, lay the hand on the mouth, and the mouth in the dust, crying out, Unclean, unclean. The more lowly thy bed, when the humility is such as the Spirit of God produces, the brighter may be thy hopes, and the higher will thy exaltation be. There are many now in glory who were once ashamed even to look to the place where God's honor dwells.

THE PROOF.

"For godly sorrow worketh repentance to salvation not to be repented of: but the sorrow of the world worketh death." — 2 Cor. vii. 10.

THE PRAYER.

"O strike this rock, that tears at length may flow,
For sins committed against love like thine;
Come, Spirit, breathe — O lay the rebel low,
Till prostrate homage own thy power divine."

Jesus.

"THOU SHALT CALL HIS NAME JESUS, FOR HE SHALL SAVE HIS PEOPLE FROM THEIR SINS." — *Matt.* i. 21.

AN infinite antidote for an infinite misery — a divine remedy for a mortal disease — a Saviour for the lost — a blessing for the accursed — life for the dying or the dead — pardon for the condemned — hope for the despairing — the image of God for those whom sin has mutilated and marred, and light for them that sit in darkness; — all these are secured for us by Him whose name is JESUS. And, O God, our Saviour, what shall we render unto thee for the great things thus accomplished for us! Surely it is our reasonable service to dedicate ourselves, souls and bodies, to thy glory. Hast thou purchased freedom? Then shall we turn it into licentiousness?

Hast thou made an end of transgression? Then shall we go on to pile sin upon sin?

Hast thou imparted spiritual health? And shall we prolong or augment the disease?

Hast thou rolled away the condemnation? Then shall we gather clouds and thick darkness again around the soul?

Is the light of God's countenance shining on us again? Then shall we extinguish that light, and walk in darkness still?

Rather, may the Spirit of all grace be shed abroad upon our hearts, that holiness to the Lord may reign there — that the love of God may preside over all — and that the work of preparation for the everlasting glory may be advancing in the soul. Nor need there be one hour's delay as to the method by which that is to be accomplished. Again, and again, it should be made plain to man that his mind must be once more in harmony with God's before he can be blessed. The creature's will must be merged in the Creator's: from day to day that should be more and more the case; and just in that proportion are men enjoying happiness on earth, or preparing for happiness in heaven. Here, then, is the anchorage of the soul — let the mind of God become the mind of man, and he need not fear though an host were encamped against him.

THE PROOF.

"This is a faithful saying, and worthy of all acceptation, that Christ Jesus came into the world to save sinners; of whom I am chief." — 1 Tim. i. 15.

THE RESOLUTION.

"O Lord, I wait the promised grace;
And when thou hast forgiven,
Pardon shall lead to holiness —
The upward path to heaven."

The Cross.

"HAVING MADE PEACE THROUGH THE BLOOD OF THE CROSS." — *Col.* i. 20.

THERE are more inscriptions on the cross of Jesus than the one which was written in Hebrew, and Greek, and Latin. *Christ crucified is the wisdom of God*, is one additional inscription read by the eye of faith. He is the wisdom of God, by making provision at once to punish sin and pardon it, at once to uphold justice in untarnished purity, and to let mercy flow forth without restraint to man.

And, *Christ crucified is the power of God*, is another inscription which faith can read upon the cross — the power of God in bringing those nigh who were before afar off, in lifting souls from the verge of hell to the vestibule of heaven, and superseding enmity to the holy by love for the pure.

Behold what sin is — That is another inscription legible by the eye of faith upon the cross. Nothing but the blood of Him who was Jehovah's fellow could atone for its guilt, or wash away its pollution. How dark, then, the guilt, and how deep the malignity of the abominable thing.

And, *Behold the love of God!* is another inscription still. He so loved the world that he gave his Son to die for us.

Or finally, *See how precious is the soul,* is another. Not corruptible things like silver and gold, but the life of one who was holy, harmless, undefiled, and separate from sinners, was the ransom paid; and who will gauge the preciousness of the soul, as it is thus valued by God?

Yet, O my soul, I have been undervaluing thee; I have been ruining thee by sin, and regarding thee as of less value than some transient enjoyment, some fancied pleasure of an hour or a breath. And how am I to escape from this condemnation? Just by clinging to the cross; not to the wooden emblem which superstition presents, or upon which it doats, but to the crucified One, who made peace through the blood of the cross, who atoned for sin there, and taught the believer to glory only in the Lord, while he exclaims, "I determined not to know any thing among you save Jesus Christ, and him crucified."

THE PROOF.

"But God forbid that I should glory, save in the cross of our Lord Jesus Christ, by whom the world is crucified unto me, and I unto the world." — GAL. vi. 14.

THE HYMN.

"The glorious emblem of God's love
Is now the death of sin;
The cross conducts us to the crown —
There all our hopes begin."

The Hiding-Place.

"A MAN SHALL BE AS AN HIDING-PLACE FROM THE WIND, AND A COVERT FROM THE TEMPEST; AS RIVERS OF WATER IN A DRY PLACE; AS THE SHADOW OF A GREAT ROCK IN A WEARY LAND." — *Isaiah* xxxii. 2.

HOW mysterious that announcement must have seemed to the carnal Jew, who neither understood nor cared for understanding his own religion! That *a man* should shelter him from troubles, sudden and severe like the sweep of the tempest — what so incredible? That *a man* should refresh and gladden like rivers of water in Oriental lands — what so impossible? Or, that *a man* should be a source of safety and of joy, like the shadow of a great rock in countries where trees are rare — that must have seemed as strange and unintelligible as speech in an unknown tongue.

But to us who live in "the last times," all is transparently plain. A man, the man Christ Jesus, is now our hiding-place and shelter. When the floods come and the storms beat, we are as safe under his shadow as in a munition of rocks: he is our Rock, our fortress, and our high tower. "Immanuel, God with us," solves that and a hundred difficulties besides. He who has seen the Son has seen the Father also; and glory to God is thus beheld in closest combination with peace and safety to the sons of men.

Stand in awe, then, O my soul, and contemplate what God has wrought. Thou art exposed to the tempest of wrath — here is thy skreen. Thou dwellest in a dry parched land — here is the river which gladdens it. The sun which scorches others need inflict no damage upon thee. Nay, like a tree planted by the rivers of water, fruit unto holiness may be gathered from thee; like willows by the water-courses, thou shouldst prosper. The early and the latter rain is made sure by the promise of Him who hung the bow in the clouds as a pledge of his faithfulness for ever, and who undertakes to be the hiding-place and shield of those who trust in his word. O trust, then, in Him, for "in the Lord there is everlasting strength." The very word which commanded the universe to be is the foundation of our hope. The truth of Him who is the same yesterday, to-day, and for ever, is our guide; who, then, is he that can injure such a soul?

THE PROOF.

"The Lord is thy keeper; the Lord is thy shade upon thy right hand. The sun shall not smite thee by day, nor the moon by night." — PSALM cxxi. 5, 6.

THE ASSURANCE.

"The Lord thy God's a sun and shield,
  He'll grace and glory give;
And will withhold no good from them
  That uprightly do live."

The Sinner's Substitute.

"HE WAS WOUNDED FOR OUR TRANSGRESSIONS, HE WAS BRUISED FOR OUR INIQUITIES: THE CHASTISEMENT OF OUR PEACE WAS UPON HIM; AND WITH HIS STRIPES WE ARE HEALED." — *Isaiah* liii. 5.

HOW blessed they who can thus appropriate the results of the Saviour's atonement! He died the just for the unjust. He endured what they should have endured. The wrath of God for sin, the hiding of His countenance from the sinner, with all the woe to which sin can lead on earth — the Saviour bore when that good Shepherd laid down his life for the sheep.

But thousands never derive any benefit from that amazing plan of substitution. It is to them only the perverted occasion of augmenting their guilt; it becomes a savor of death unto death.

How blessed they, then, who can appropriate the benefits of Christ's atoning death — who can humbly say, "Christ loved me, and gave himself for me!" He was wounded for our transgressions; then divine justice will not wound *me also*. He was bruised for our iniquities; then the just God and the holy will not bruise *me also*. The chastisement of our peace was upon him; and the holy God cannot punish *me also*, for that were to punish twice for the same transgression. By his stripes we are healed; then I cannot die the second death, for Christ has tasted death for me, a believer in his name. It is thus that the believer is privileged to reason, and, O my soul, honor the Spirit, that He may thus teach thee. Let it be the business of thy earthly existence to make sure of a dwelling in the house not made with hands. Count every thing intrusive and impertinent which would hinder that work; and to stimulate thee in it, think of those who have reached the limits of their threescore years and ten with no provision for eternity, nothing on which to die, but a mere *peradventure*. When they stood as little children by their mother's knee, they knew as much of their eternity and their prospects there, as they do now, when they are within an hour or a day of their decisive meeting with their Judge! Now, can such men be wise? are they self-loving? Nay, they have forsaken their own mercies, and their case should warn us to "give diligence," as God has commanded, to "make our calling and election *sure*."

THE PROOF.

"I am crucified with Christ: nevertheless I live; yet not I, but Christ liveth in me: and the life which I now live in the flesh I live by the faith of the Son of God, who loved me, and gave himself for me." — GAL. ii. 20.

THE HYMN.

"With Christ the Lord we died to sin,
With Christ to life we rise —
A life which, now begun on earth,
Is perfect in the skies."

The Alternative.

"BUT IF OUR GOSPEL BE HID, IT IS HID TO THEM THAT ARE LOST: IN WHOM THE GOD OF THIS WORLD HATH BLINDED THE MINDS OF THEM WHICH BELIEVE NOT, LEST THE LIGHT OF THE GLORIOUS GOSPEL OF CHRIST, WHO IS THE IMAGE OF GOD, SHINE UNTO THEM."—2 *Cor.* iv. 3, 4.

A SAVOR of life unto life, or of death unto death: such is the alternative put solemnly before us by the God of the gospel, the God and Father of our Lord Jesus Christ. When welcomed, the gospel becomes a savor of life unto life — it brings life from the living God, and imparts it to us, teaching us to say, "I live, yet not I, but Christ liveth in me." But when it is rejected, the gospel becomes the perverted cause of the second death; the soul is left to remediless woe for ever. "There remaineth no more sacrifice for sin, but a certain fearful looking for of judgment."

My soul, how is it with thee? Hast thou welcomed the gospel in spirit and in truth, or hast thou only fawned upon it, while in thy heart thou couldst trample upon it, and despise all its dowry of glories? O do not forget that if the gospel seem a dark and a mysterious thing to thee, it is because thou art lost, God being witness. If its glories have not won thy love for the true God, it is because thou art a dupe of the god of this world. If God's last dispensation for the saving of sinners have failed to produce the desired effect in thee, then be not deceived, God is not mocked; what thou sowest thou must reap — either the light of the glorious gospel of Christ, or the blackness of darkness for ever; either the Son of God received and rested on, or everlasting destruction from the presence of the Lord; either an interest in Him of whom you read "fury is not in me," or "the fiery indignation which shall consume the adversaries."

And is it not a cause of joy that the gospel is so simple in itself? Men may argue and dispute, till the very truth of God seem to become a questionable thing; but, amid all that, the gospel in all its unutterable simplicity remains still the same. It does not consist in a doctrine, nor a series of doctrines. These may be welcomed, and yet the gospel may remain unfelt. It is all contained *in Christ*, and the receiving of Him is the grand turning point in the history of every saved soul.

THE PROOF.

"If we sin wilfully after that we have received the knowledge of the truth, there remaineth no more sacrifice for sins, but a certain fearful looking for of judgment and fiery indignation, which shall devour the adversaries." — HEB. x. 26, 27.

THE PRAYER.

"Lord, I am thine by countless ties,
  Thine I would ever be;
O by thy Spirit mould my soul,
  That I may live for Thee."

The Force of Truth.

"FOR THE WORD OF GOD IS QUICK, AND POWERFUL, AND SHARPER THAN ANY TWO-EDGED SWORD, PIERCING EVEN TO THE DIVIDING ASUNDER OF SOUL AND SPIRIT, AND OF THE JOINTS AND MARROW, AND IS A DISCERNER OF THE THOUGHTS AND INTENTS OF THE HEART."—*Heb.* iv. 12.

GOD has magnified his Word above all his name. It is his chosen instrument for reclaiming a world to himself, and stamping the beauties of holiness upon those who are now covered with wounds, and bruises, and noisome sores.

Now, that Word is *quick*. It is a living thing. It proves its vitality and vigor by the fact, that it either warns man to flee from the wrath to come, or, if the warning be slighted, becomes a savor of death unto death.

It is *powerful* also. Men may resist it, or attempt to dash it from them, but still it holds them fast; it either drags them to judgment, or directs them to the cross.

And it is *sharper than any two-edged sword*. Such a sword can mutilate and mangle the body; it cannot touch the soul. But the sword of the Spirit, which is the Word of God, pierces even to the dividing asunder of the soul and the spirit. It separates what man possesses in common with the beasts which perish, or mere animal life, from that which he may enjoy in common with Godhead, or spiritual life. Like the all-seeing Eye, it penetrates everywhere, and it pierces every thing.

Moreover, it is a *discerner of the thoughts and intents of the heart.* It detects the sinner; it unmasks the hypocrite, while, like the father of the prodigal, it sees the penitent though still a great way off — it takes him by the hand; it speaks words to his heart, and guides him to the spot where his God and he walk together again like those who are agreed. In accomplishing all that, it may operate like the surgeon's knife, dividing asunder the joints and marrow; but the pain is salutary, and spiritual health is the result when the Spirit blesses the means. Is it true, then, that my soul has felt that keen edge, and said, Let the righteous smite me? Is it true that the Word of God is my soul's daily bread, or the man of its right hand? Then God has visited, and the entrance of his Word has given light — it will do for the soul what it was blessed to do for the world in apostolic times, and again at the Reformation, when the churches rejoiced in the truth of God, and rejected the lies of man.

THE PROOF.

"Thy word is a lamp unto my feet, and a light unto my path." — PSALM cxix. 105.

THE HYMN.

"Precious Book! of books the best,
The dearest gift of God but one:
That surpasses all the rest —
The gift of God's beloved Son."

The Glory of Man.

"THE SUN SHALL BE NO MORE THY LIGHT BY DAY; NEITHER FOR BRIGHTNESS SHALL THE MOON GIVE LIGHT UNTO THEE: BUT THE LORD SHALL BE UNTO THEE AN EVERLASTING LIGHT, AND THY GOD THY GLORY." — *Isaiah* lx. 19.

THE aching void which sin has left within the soul of man is to be filled up by the friendship of God; it could be filled up by nothing less. The prophet saw what was needed, at once by the Church and the individual believer; and in his own glowing strains, announces what it is that constitutes our glory, namely, our God.

Our God — not the idols on which we are prone to rest, as if they could meet the demands of a being like man's soul, created for eternal duration, and for boundless blessedness.

Our God — and not our own handiwork, proud as we are of such transient or polluted things.

Our God himself — and not the works even of his hands, glorious though they be, and reflective of his wisdom, his goodness, and power. Not the sea, that type of his immensity; not the sky, the most dazzling of his works; not the earth, stored as it is with his bounty; but Himself, in all his perfections — his love, his compassion, and his mercy to man. Now, could the thought be entertained of an angel flitting from star to star, and trying to find in each some new form of glory, is it likely that he would ever discover aught to eclipse the appointed glory of the believer — his God? There, then, let the soul rest — there let it be at peace, at perfect peace: it is still a blind and a degraded thing, if its God do not yield it joy.

But how is all this verified? In a way which is at once exquisitely simple and unspeakably gladdening. Every thing that the believer has (except indwelling sin) is God's. Has he righteousness? It is the righteousness of God. Has he hope? It is hope in God. Has he peace? It is the peace of God. Has he joy? It is joy in God. And has he glory? "Thy God thy glory," is the Divine reply. Such is the provision made to satisfy the believer's soul; and surely on that he may repose, and enjoy the peace, while he delights in the smile, of his God. And now, my soul, how is it with thee? Hast thou learned to soar, or art thou still grovelling in the dust? Is God thy glory, and thy joy, or is some perishing thing all that thou hast to satisfy the vast desires of the heart?

THE PROOF.

"My soul shall make her boast in the LORD. The humble shall hear thereof, and be glad." — PSALM xxxiv. 2.

THE HYMN.

"Earth's beauties blending all in one,
  Were but an infant's toy;
For nobler things man's spirit pants —
  His God must be his joy."

The Sun of Righteousness.

"UNTO YOU THAT FEAR MY NAME SHALL THE SUN OF RIGHTEOUSNESS ARISE WITH HEALING IN HIS WINGS." —*Mal.* iv. 2.

THE mercies of God, in all their amplitude, are freely offered to all. Barbarian, Scythian, bond and free, are all welcome; nay, all are pressed to close with the Holy One's offers. Expostulation, remonstrance, and melting entreaty, are each in turn employed to prevail on the sinner to return to God and live.

But free as these mercies are in the offer of them to all, the Bible is ever circumspect and cautious as to those who *actually enjoy* the benefits thus presented. No happiness for man while living in sin, and no mercy till he forsake it by fleeing to Christ. No promises fulfilled in any saving sense while man exists in a state of revolt from God. Before any saving blessing can be enjoyed, a certain character must be possessed. It is written, for example, "Unto *you that fear my name* shall the Sun of Righteousness arise with healing in his wings," and there is no light, no healing, no spiritual joy, for any others. I must come to Christ before I get the promised rest. I must seek as God commands, ere I can find, as God has guaranteed in his Word.

And how blessed the assurance which we have

here! The Sun, and that the Sun of Righteousness, arising! At sunrise all nature seems to revive. The mountains, first tipped with light, speed on the glad intelligence to the valley, and nature is forthwith all a-glow. Now, what happens on the visible landscape when the sun arises, and towers, and rocks, and streams, and waving woods, all start from twilight into sunshine, takes place in the soul when the Sun of Righteousness arises upon man. All becomes radiant now. The darkness of nature is slowly dispelled; and as the soul sees light in God's light, it rejoices more and more in the effulgence. O how suicidal is man, who prefers darkness to that, and often plunges into sin, lest the true light should irradiate and save! My soul, let the dust be thy bed, and sackcloth thy covering, because thou didst once love darkness; but let thy life be henceforth to the praise of Him who has now "made thee to differ."

THE PROOF.

"Light is sown for the righteous, and gladness for the upright in heart." — Psalm xcvii. 11.

THE HYMN.

"How majestic the scene when at day-dawn the sun,
  Careering in glory, sails slow on the view!
 Yet deeper the bliss when the Sun of the soul
  Sheds his lustre on men, all their powers to renew."

Spiritual Declension.

"FROM THAT TIME MANY OF HIS DISCIPLES WENT BACK, AND WALKED NO MORE WITH HIM."— *John* vi. 66.

WERE the believer's life a sail upon a summer sea — did no clouds ever gather, or no tempest break — such a life would be hailed by multitudes. Were there no duties which cross the purposes of man, no truths which humble him, no convictions which show that he is by nature " poor, and wretched and miserable, and blind, and naked," all would welcome a system so easy; they would rejoice in the Saviour's light.

But when His religion comes with sorrow and self-denial in its train, few cordially embrace it; they offer it only the semblance of homage. They weary of watching; they will not pray always; they reach a point where they abandon the truth; they make shipwreck of the faith and a good conscience; they once put their hands to the plough, but they now look back, and soon learn to walk without the fear of God, as the world does.

There are cases, however, in which the apostasy is not final. The soul is reclaimed; it is moved to return and do its first works, and like Peter after his fall, it is raised up by the very hand which it had forsaken. And O, how pungent the sorrows which often follow these temporary declensions! Before the soul be restored to its former rank, the bitter tears of Peter are often shed. Woes are endured like those of him who once denied the faith, and signed a deed to that effect, but who was eventually restored, then died a martyr to the truth, and in testimony of his compunction thrust his right hand into the flames, that the member with which he had sinned might be the first that was consumed.

Now, is my soul watching against all such declensions? Is it my endeavor and my prayer to be steadfast and unmovable, always abounding in the work of the Lord? Am I impressed, as every self-loving soul should be, with the solemn warning, "If any man draw back, my soul shall have no pleasure in him?" All that is tender in the love, or terrible in the justice of God, pleads for steadfast adherence to the Lord our righteousness; all that is precious in the soul points in the same direction, while the joy of the Lord is the promised portion of those who follow on to know him.

THE PROOF.

"Ephraim shall say, What have I to do any more with idols." — HOSEA xiv. 8.

THE CONVICTION.

"Draw back! Nay, onward, upward still
 Must be the heavenward way;
Ten thousand dangers need not daunt —
 God is our strength and stay."

The Great Restoration.

"BUT WILL GOD IN VERY DEED DWELL WITH MEN ON THE EARTH?"—2 *Chron.* vi. 18.

WE often hear the sad story of children who have wandered from their father's home. They may have ventured rashly on the deep, and been drifted out to sea; or they may have strayed into the forest, and there become entangled so as to be in danger of death; or they may have lost their way amid the streets and the lanes of some vast city, and cannot tell either their name or their father's abode. But O how glad when they are once more restored to their parents' sheltering roof — how welcome the smile of the familiar faces, and how speedily the tear is dried!

Now, something of the same kind has happened to wayward man. The children of our Father who is in heaven have wandered away from his shelter and his love, along ten thousand paths. So long have they strayed, that they have lost all knowledge of the way; and, in their misdirected efforts to regain it, ten thousand times ten thousand are wandering farther and farther still. Some bemoan themselves in their sad condition; but many, like the prodigal before he came to himself, appear to deem that their joy or their freedom, which is, in reality, their bondage and their woe.

But back to his God man must be guided; or, like the

"Tribes of the wandering foot and weary breast,"

he is necessarily wretched. And how can man get back to God? The whole Bible is a reply. When we could neither ascend to him, nor yet be happy without him, He came down to us. In very deed he dwelt with man on the earth; and now the brightness of his glory gladdens, the plenitude of his mercy saves, through Jesus Christ our Lord. Behold the consummation of heavenly wisdom, and O, my soul, rejoice in it as also the consummation of thy joy. What seemed only a dim conjecture or a distant hope in the days of Solomon, was turned into a blessed reality eighteen centuries and a half ago; and now, man once degraded and prostrate, may be erect and ennobled again. To "walk with Christ in newness of life," is the end of all perfection.

THE PROOF.

"We have redemption through Christ's blood, even the forgiveness of sins: who is the image of the invisible God. . . . ."— Col. i. 14, 15.

THE HYMN.

"No more let me doat as if earth were my home;
It is only the place of my exile and woe:
From all that can gladden I thoughtlessly roam,
Till the God, who in mercy redeemed me, I know."

The Heart-Searcher.

"NEITHER IS THERE ANY CREATURE THAT IS NOT MANIFEST IN HIS SIGHT: BUT ALL THINGS ARE NAKED AND OPENED UNTO THE EYES OF HIM WITH WHOM WE HAVE TO DO."—*Heb.* iv. 13.

THERE are many sentences in the Word of God brief and simple, but so thoroughly charged with meaning, that, if even one of them were made the universal rule of conduct, it would revolutionize the moral world. So fully, in many cases, does even a single clause embody the mind of God, that, if it were to become the mind of man, he that is filthy would cease to be filthy any more; he that now loves a lie would become enamoured of the truth; and a new moral beauty would be spread in the life, and among the homes of men.

The text of our present meditation is such a portion of the Word—it is felt to be like a glance of the Heart-searcher's eye, if the conscience be quick, and the soul an object of interest. "There is no creature that is not manifest in his sight." The most microscopic and the most mighty object in creation are equally exposed to His scrutiny. Especially does he look man's heart through and through; he turns over all its folds, and follows it through all its windings, insomuch that there is not a thought in the heart, but, lo, he knows it altogether. Every sin is committed in God's presence. He is a witness to it; so that the sinner, in effect, challenges the judgment of God.

And "all things are naked and opened unto his eyes." There is no darkness, and no disguise to him. Even our secret sins are set in the light of his countenance; and were one of them to pass unpunished, that much would be subtracted from the perfection of his justice.

But finally, "*we have to do*" with that Heart-searcher, and these simple words are full of significance. We must meet him face to face. We must give in our account to Him in person for the deeds done in the body; and who may abide that ordeal? Out of Christ, who shall stand when the throne of judgment is set? O my soul, make sure of the constituted Advocate with the Father, Jesus Christ the righteous. With Him as thy Shepherd, no evil need be heeded; but every other protection is a refuge of lies, a gourd when the scorching sun arises.

THE PROOF.

"O Lord, thou hast searched me, and known me. Thou knowest my down-sitting and mine up-rising: thou understandest my thought afar off." — PSALM cxxxix. 1, 2.

THE HYMN.

"No darkness screens us from the gaze
Of Godhead's flame-bright eye;
It pierces through the densest haze,
And gleams where'er we fly."

The Arm of the Lord.

"AND GIDEON CAME TO JORDAN, AND PASSED OVER, HE, AND THE THREE HUNDRED MEN THAT WERE WITH HIM, FAINT, YET PURSUING THEM."—*Judges* viii. 4.

THE attitude of Gideon and his little band is one which the believer should often study; that warrior's case is often ours in the good fight of faith.

"I am weary and faint in my mind," one may exclaim. Then think of Gideon, and pursue even amid your fainting.

"I shall one day perish," is the fear of another. Then fall with the face to the enemy, and conquer even in dying, as the Redeemer did.

"There is a lion in the way, a lion in the streets," is the conviction of a third. Such lions flee when we assail them; a man may put a thousand to flight, if he will only grasp the shield of faith and the sword of the Spirit.

"Unstable as water, I cannot excel," is the complaint of another. Then lean the more upon Him who can make the weak to be like David.

"My sins appear more numerous and vile from day to day," is the deep and the painful feeling of others. Then away to the fountain opened for sin and for uncleanness. Haste and flee for your life.

"They of my own house are my enemies," exclaims another, "and I am hindered when I would advance." Appeal the more frequently to Him who is the friend of the sinner, and the guide of the perplexed.

"I am prone every hour to sink back to the world," is another complaint. True; but do you not know of one who said, "Be of good cheer, for I have overcome the world," and who overcame it for you, if you believe? If your own strength be your confidence, you will soon sink indeed. If Jehovah be your strength, who is he that will harm you?

"Can I be a child of God," one asks, "while sin is so strong in my soul?" — The Scriptures suggest for an answer — Paul was forced to exclaim, under the pressure of indwelling sin, "O wretched man that I am, who shall deliver me from the body of this death?" and was taught by the Spirit to reply, "I thank God through Jesus Christ our Lord."

Like the autumn leaves for number, are the sorrows and the trials of a believer; but One in whom all the fulness of the Godhead bodily dwells has come: He is with us always to save and sustain. Away, then, with all complaints, as if the Lord could forsake us; let every fear drive us nearer to Him, and perfect love will cast out fear.

THE PROOF.

"Who is he that will harm you, if ye be the followers of that which is good?" — 1 Pet. iii. 13.

THE HYMN.

"Does Hermon's dew fall sweet at eve?
So Jesus soothes the weary saint.
Do palm tree shades make deserts glad?
So Jesus cheers us when we faint."

The Stronghold.

"SURELY THERE IS NO ENCHANTMENT AGAINST JACOB, NEITHER IS THERE ANY DIVINATION AGAINST ISRAEL."—*Num.* xxiii. 23.

THE Word of God is full of the strongest assurances of a believer's safety. So numerous are they, that our religion falls short of what it was designed to be, if we are not reposing in serenity and peace, under Almighty protection. We are to be kept "in perfect peace," if we act on the heavenly terms. The name of the Lord is a strong tower, into which the righteous should run and be safe. There is a sure foundation laid in Zion, and he that builds upon it shall never be put to shame. In six troubles, yea, in seven, the Lord is to be our stay. He is our sun and shield. When we pass through the waters he will be with us, and through the rivers they shall not overflow us; when we walk through the fire we shall not be burnt, neither shall the flame kindle upon us.— But we must transcribe a large portion of the Bible, if we would detail its assurances of safety to the believer. They are numerous, like the stars of the midnight sky.

Balaam felt the truth of all this, when he said, "There is no enchantment against Jacob, nor any divination against Israel." He was willing to curse them for hire; but there was a hand which held him back — it was as if his tongue cleaved to the roof of his mouth, when he tried to curse those whom the Lord had blessed. The mighty shield was over them, and the hireling recoiled from doing the work for which the bribe was offered. Though Balak had given him a house full of gold, Balaam could not go beyond the Word of God, to do less or more.

And it is still the same with those whose stronghold is the Lord. The humblest of his saints is the object of his care, though unbelief may often doubt it. There is not one among the sons of men, if he have come to the fountain open for sin, who is not thus under an almighty Guardian's shelter. Even my sin-laden soul may be so, unless I prefer some refuge of lies to the "hiding-place from the storm." O flee, then, to that hiding-place, and dwell in perfect peace.

THE PROOF.

"And the work of righteousness shall be peace; and the effect of righteousness, quietness and assurance for ever. And my people shall dwell in a peaceable habitation, and in sure dwellings, and in quiet resting-places." — ISAIAH xxxii. 17, 18.

THE HYMN.

"The Son of God in love became
 Peace to the sons of men —
The blood which cleanses sin away,
 Awakes their joy again.

"Serenely safe, they now repose
 Beneath a heavenly shade;
And smile to heaven in love again,
 For woes so well allayed."

THE WONDERS OF REDEEMING LOVE.

744296

THE WONDERS OF REDEEMING LOVE.

The Wonderful.

"HIS NAME SHALL BE CALLED WONDERFUL." — *Isaiah* ix. 6.

WHO shall recount the wonders of which He is the substance and the sum? The guiltless dies for the guilty. Weakness is combined with Omnipotence. Purity and suffering are seen together, each in the supreme degree. Justice and mercy meet and embrace. Pardon for the sinner — and yet the utmost penalty of the law against the sin. Grace to help — and therefore strength for those who are by nature unstable as water. The righteousness of God to justify, and the peace of God to enjoy — a pure conscience where sin has been like scarlet and crimson — Godhead and humanity walking hand in hand among the sons of men — omnipotence to shield — love to comfort — compassion to pity — patience to bear with — wisdom to guide — goodness to supply our wants; — these and countless other mercies meet in Immanuel,

"*The Wonderful,*" and such is the provision made by God over all to meet the wants of the soul, and rescue it from perdition. My soul, art thou rescued — or dost thou still cling to ruin? He who seeks thy ruin is called *Legion;* but He who came to save is *The Wonderful:* O cling to Him; rest on Him, and there rejoice for ever. Never forget for a day, or an hour, that by that plan of wonderful mercy, of which the Saviour is at once the author and the sum, every sin we have committed is a reason why we should flee to Him. Conscience bids us stand aloof. The law enforces the suggestion; and, while we have no guide but these, the most we can do is to fear and quake on the one hand, or be dead and indifferent upon the other. It is when we see the law magnified, conscience purified, and the Holy One in Christ beckoning us to glory, that we begin to sing of mercy — it is then that we learn that the half has not been told concerning the Wonderful One.

THE PROOF.

"In Him are hid all the treasures of wisdom and knowledge." — Col. ii. 3.

THE HYMN.

"His name shall be the Prince of Peace,
For evermore adored,
The *Wonderful,* the Counsellor,
The great and mighty Lord."

1*

The Two Pleas.

"FOR THY NAME'S SAKE, O LORD, PARDON MINE INIQUITY; FOR IT IS GREAT."—*Psalm* xxv. 11.

AMONG the wonders of redeeming love we should not fail to notice the pleas which the sinner is warranted to employ. Pardon is the thing required: till that be obtained, the soul is wretched, and every living soul accordingly pants or clamors for it.

Now, mark the argument which it urges—"For Thy name's sake" is the first. God's glory—the praise of the glory of his grace—is supremely kept in view by the Spirit-taught soul; not man's merit, but the glory of God's sovereign name is the all-prevailing plea.

But in the matter of pardon, man does find a plea in himself—and what is it? *The greatness of his sin.* It is so great that it crushes him to the dust. He cannot lie under it and live. He therefore at once confesses its magnitude, and cries for deliverance on that very account. O how prevailing this confession is! how humbling to the sinner! how glorifying to the God of pardons! how full of sweetness and soothing to the contrite soul! The law says the greatness of sin is a source of despair; the gospel says the greatness of sin is a reason why you should flee to God for hope—and eye hath not seen, nor ear heard, the blessedness of him who has thus fled like a prisoner of hope to the stronghold of the gospel.

There is a struggling soul. It has found out what it is to be a sinner, and it is weighed down to the dust; in that condition many have meditated, and some have attempted, self-destruction. But now it has advanced a step farther — it is led by the Spirit to the cross; faith like a mustard seed appears; hope begins to dawn; again it is eclipsed; then it brightens — it is like a little boat upon an angry sea, now tipping the wave, and then plunging into the abyss, as if it had gone down. All the while, however, the sense of sin is pressing that soul nearer to the Saviour. Sin, Satan, the deceitful heart, all whisper there is no hope; but faith grasps the promise — "Though your sins were like scarlet, ye shall be white as snow;" and reposing upon that, it is glad.

THE PROOF.

"Who is a God like unto thee, that pardoneth iniquity, and passeth by the transgression of the remnant of his heritage?" — MICAH vii. 18.

THE PRAYER.

"Now for thine own name's sake, O Lord,
   I humbly thee entreat
To pardon mine iniquity,
   For it is very great."

The Reign of Love.

"THE LOVE OF CHRIST CONSTRAINETH US."—2 *Cor.* v. 14.

ALL that God had done for man had failed to win his heart. Gift upon gift, till the number could not be counted, had been showered upon him. The riches of nature had been poured into his lap. In some lands, the year was one unceasing autumn — but all was unavailing. Man forgot the Giver while luxuriating in the gift.

But, after all, He who is love cannot abandon man; and when all else had failed, another, a last, alternative is tried. The love of God in Christ is revealed — and man's heart is captivated: his affections are now set on things above. The law, with its terrors, could not succeed. Providence, with its ever full and ever-flowing stream of bounties, could not avail. Creation, with all that is stupendous in its wonders, or wise in its adaptations, was no less unavailing — man was still stout-hearted and far from righteousness. But a new moral power was revealed — an influence was employed which man could not both feel and resist. Something was made known which can change the wolf or the lion into a lamb — which can elevate the degraded, and purify the vile, as well as gladden the downcast. It was the love of God in Christ. It was the amazing display made upon the cross; and that is slowly linking all the nations of the world into one, as it links all the redeemed to the cross of Christ and the throne of the Eternal.

How greatly blessed are they who have felt that ove, and who love in return! How greatly blessed they who have learned to testify their love by imitating Him who loved them and gave himself for them! O my soul, let the prayer from day to day ascend, that the Spirit of love may be more and more shed abroad in thee and in the world. It is thus that Eden is restored, and thus that God and man walk together again, even as they did before the fall. Ere man can be blessed again, he must regain what he forfeited by sinning. He can no more be happy without the image and the friendship of God, than flesh and blood can find their native element in the consuming fire. The grand result of redemption, therefore, is to restore that image and that favor. When that is accomplished, the object of Christ's death is realized. The love of Christ is ascendant, and man is on the way to blessedness for ever.

THE PROOF.

"Herein is love, not that we loved God, but that he loved us, and sent his Son to be the propitiation for our sins."— 1 JOHN iv. 10.

THE HYMN.

" What is freedom to the captive?
   Life to man when doomed to die?
More glad the love of Heaven
   To the mourner's upward eye."

The Wonder of Wonders.

"GOD BE MERCIFUL TO ME A SINNER." — *Luke* xviii. 13.

AMONG the chief marvels over which the believer rejoices, when the Spirit of God has enlightened him, is the fact that salvation is provided *for sinners*. The publican's prayer embodies the truth; and could we be brought cordially to urge that prayer, the soul would soon be blessed. It is to me, a sinner, that mercy is offered; if I were not a sinner, I would not need it, and it is the wonder of wonders that the righteousness of God is so declared in the gospel, that he is just in the very act of justifying sinners who believe. While protesting with a voice far more loud than thunder against all iniquity, they are yet the guilty, the condemned, the lost, whom the God of the gospel contemplates. Self-righteousness thinks it should be otherwise, and the Pharisee of every age cries out against such a scheme. But the righteous Lord, who loveth righteousness, has adopted it, at once to raise the fallen and deepen the hosannas of the saved.

Look, then, my soul — as a sinner, look to Christ, and be saved. Try to look, on the ground that thou art a believer — that is, make thy faith the source of hope; and that faith is made thy Saviour, while Christ is dishonored. But disown all else, that

Christ may be every thing to thee. Come as a sinner — come again as a sinner, and again and again. In a word, employ the publican's prayer — let it come from the heart, and then beauty will be given for ashes, the oil of joy for mourning, while the very righteousness of God becomes the garment of the soul.

Nor need you ever fear that this will diminish your obligations to be holy. Who so thoroughly bound to die to sin, as those who believe in Him who died for it? That conviction should press us ever upwards in the path of duty. Purity, like that of Christ, should be the believer's aim; and it is the sure decree of God, that we can no more see the Lord without holiness, than approach the Father otherwise than through the Son.

THE PROOF.

"And every man that hath this hope in him purifieth himself, even as He is pure." — 1 JOHN iii. 3

THE HYMN

"' Ho, ye that thirst!' behold the cry
  Of heavenly love to man;
'Come *with* the burden *for* relief,'
  Lo, Heaven's benignant plan.

"Then let the thirsty soul, refreshed,
  Haste on its holy way:
Shall blood-bought souls, enslaved again,
  Their Saviour disobey?"

The God of Pardons.

"WHO IS A GOD LIKE UNTO THEE, THAT PARDONETH INIQUITY, AND PASSETH BY THE TRANSGRESSION OF THE REMNANT OF HIS HERITAGE? HE RETAINETH NOT HIS ANGER FOR EVER, BECAUSE HE DELIGHTETH IN MERCY."—*Micah* vii. 18.

THE wonder is that God should ever pardon a single sin. His declaration in the beginning was in effect, "The soul that sinneth shall die;" and mere reason or mere conscience knows nothing of any other verdict: it cannot even appreciate God's plan of pardon when it has been announced. But when we have been taught to understand how freely God can pardon iniquity — how honoring are the terms on which he can blot out our sins, although they be like crimson and like scarlet — then the soul exults in the discovery more than they that divide the spoil. "He pardoneth iniquity;" nay more, "He passeth by the transgression of the remnant of his heritage;" nay more, "He retaineth not his anger for ever;" and the reason is, "He delighteth in mercy." All this imparts a knowledge to the soul, which spreads gladness there, as streams in the desert are fringed with verdure and fertility. Some of our race, who are born to trouble as the sparks fly upward, groan under the burden of poverty; others are vexed by protracted disease; some are afflicted in those whom they love, so that their enemies are often they of their own house;

others still are tried by the faithlessness of friendship, when those in whom they confide prove like a summer brook, or like waters that fail. But there is a burden heavier far than these, which pains and oppresses the soul that is convicted of sin — the burden of guilt, and the pain of defilement; and it is when the means of escape from that burden and that pollution are first revealed to the mind, that the soul is truly blessed. Its name is no longer Hephzibah, but Buelah, for the Lord delights in it, and it delights in the Lord. His glory is now its great object, and it is now His peculiar care. That soul has almighty strength to lean upon, and omniscience to consult; and thus furnished by the grace of God for all that can befall, it cries with Paul in his chains at Rome, "I can do all things through Christ who strengtheneth me."

THE PROOF.

"He will turn again, he will have compassion upon us; he will subdue our iniquities; and thou wilt cast all their sins into the depths of the sea." — MICAH vii. 19.

THE HYMN.

"The sun above shall fade at last,
  The heavens shall haste away,
The ocean shall desert his bed,
  Earth's glories all decay.

"For sun, and sky, and sea, and land,
  Are creatures doomed to perish;
But, changeless as the throne of God,
  The hopes his saints may cherish."

Pardon and its Fruit.

"NATHAN SAID UNTO DAVID, THE LORD HATH PUT AWAY THY SIN."—2 *Sam.* xii. 13.

"MY SIN IS EVER BEFORE ME."—*Psalm* li. 3.

THESE two portions of the Word of God display another peculiarity in that religion of which love is the origin and consummation. The Lord blots out iniquity. He does not remember transgression: when he comes near to a soul in mercy, he expunges its guilt—it is sought for and nowhere to be found. But that soul cannot forgive itself. Nay, its cry now is, "I was as a beast before thee." I can neither forget nor forgive myself for committing the abominable thing. And against *whom* have I transgressed? That God who blots out iniquity like a cloud. Or, again; against *what* have I transgressed? That justice which is the pillar at once of the throne of God and of the universe which he has made; that compassion which bore with me amid a thousand waywardnesses, and that mercy which is over all God's other works. O, surely the dust is my becoming bed; and all the more lowly should I lie because God has put away the iniquity of may sins. Conscience now testifies, according to the gospel, that there is no condemnation from God; but just the deeper is my condemnation from myself. The law of holiness is met and magnified: but the new law of love is just the more constraining.

Be the dust, then, my bed, and be sackcloth my covering there; but, at the same time, let radiant hope animate my soul — let holy boldness guide my steps — when I read so brightly in the pages of the gospel, "The Lord hath put away thy sin." Its condemning power is over, though it may still humble, and vex, and pain. There is much reason for walking circumspectly, and we may well blush and be ashamed; but if the Lord be "pacified towards us," then we may lift up the hands that hang down; we may take with us words, and return unto the living God. In that, our safety and our peace are found, for He will redeem his promise — "They that wait upon the Lord shall renew their strength; they shall mount up with wings as eagles; they shall run, and not be weary; and they shall walk, and not faint."

THE PROOF.

"They shall not be ashamed that wait for me." — ISAIAH xlix. 23.

THE HYMN.

"O, shall we not exulting flee,
When God invites us near?
The open fountain waits to cleanse,
The God of grace to cheer.

"A radiant mercy, deep as floods,
Flows from his lofty throne,
And love, like sunlight, shines on all
Whose trust is Christ alone."

Abased, yet Hoping.

"WHAT IS MAN, THAT THOU ART MINDFUL OF HIM? AND THE SON OF MAN THAT THOU VISITEST HIM?" — *Psalm* viii. 4.

SO mindful as to lift him from the dust that he may sit with princes! So mindful as to send his own Son to suffer and to die in man's stead! So mindful as to commission the Spirit of all grace to take up his abode in man's heart, and there make all things new! So mindful as to stamp God's image on the soul again, and fit it for glory, honor, and immortality!

The believing apprehension of these and similar truths often fills the soul with amazement. All this for me! Such mercy, such glory for me! Such affluence of wisdom put forth to rescue me! Such thoughts sometimes prompt the soul to question the whole scheme of redemption, as the disciples questioned the Redeemer's resurrection, because "they could not believe it for joy." But when the soul falls back on the Word of God, when it reads line upon line in favor of self-ruined man, then, if that soul be a believing one, its wonder is expressed as David expressed his, and there is no tinge of doubt in the expression. The mouth of the Lord has spoken his loving-kindness to the sons of men. The death of the Saviour shows us the very heart of Jehovah; and rejoicing in his love, the believer blesses the merciful One who remembered him in his lost condition, and said, "Deliver from going down to the pit, for I have found a ransom." It is then that man begins to see the full meaning of the words, that the Lord is to the soul what the early and the latter rain is to the fruits of the field — that He is like the dew to Israel — that He is a sun and a shield — and will withhold no good from those who seek him in spirit and in truth. O my soul, is it thus with thee? Does He whose eyes behold and whose eyelids try the children of men, see thee at once deeply abased, yet humbly hoping — at once admiring his mercy and confiding in it? Then, let the new song be in thy mouth, even praise to our God. He has visited and redeemed thee. The second death is over. Thou hast a part in the first resurrection.

THE PROOF.

"O the depth of the riches both of the wisdom and knowledge of God! how unsearchable are his judgments, and his ways past finding out!" — ROMANS xi. 33.

THE HYMN.

"When all thy mercies, O my God!
　My rising soul surveys,
Transported with the view, I'm lost
　In wonder, love, and praise.

"Thy Son, my substitute and hope;
　His agonies my bliss;
His death my life, his grave my hope,
　His heaven my happiness."

The Sure Defence.

"THE LORD OF HOSTS IS WITH US; THE GOD OF JACOB IS OUR REFUGE."—*Psalm* xlvi. 7.

HE might have been emptying the vials of His wrath upon us. He might have abandoned us when we had abandoned Him, and left us to be filled with the fruits of our own devices. As we had sowed the wind, He might have left us to reap the whirlwind; and His justice would still have been untarnished. But mercy rejoices over judgment, and "the Lord of hosts is with us; the God of Jacob is our refuge." He is at our right hand, and we cannot be greatly moved. Temptation comes; but need it prevail when the Lord of hosts is on our side? Trials may be multiplied; but need they ever overwhelm us when Omnipotence is our stay? Satan may buffet. Though he cannot destroy a believer's *soul*, he may mar his *peace;* yet even in that he need not succeed, since the God of Jacob is our refuge. He who leads Joseph like a flock will defend and guard his own; and the result will be glory to Him who always causes us to triumph. "Greater is He that is for us than all that can be against us," may now become the believer's song, and may constitute a portion of his praises on earth, preparatory to his singing the song of Moses and the Lamb for ever.

Here, then, the devout believer may exclaim, here is the rock of my refuge — here is my safe and quiet retreat; whatever may befall, hither I will flee, and there can be no overthrow when I have the mighty God of Jacob for my defence; there need not be even a wound while I hold the shield of faith, yea, while the Lord God himself is my shield. Enter then, O my soul, on thy peace. Do not rob the Prince of Peace of his glory, as if he would forsake or could not defend thee. Thy God is now thy all; thy righteousness, to justify; thy peace, to tranquillize; thy hope, to animate; and at last,

> "Though every form of death and every woe
> Shot from malignant stars to earth below,"

thy portion to enjoy for ever.

THE PROOF.

"And the rain descended, and the floods came, and the winds blew, and beat upon that house; and it fell not: for it was founded upon a rock." — MATT. vii. 25.

THE HYMN.

> "As Noah saw the waters swell,
> To sweep a world away;
> Yet gazed undaunted on the storm,
> His God, his hope, and stay:
>
> "So Faith, amid a thousand ills,
> Clings to creative might;
> And, shielded by Omnipotence,
> Smiles welcome to the fight."

The Name of the Lord.

"THE LORD PASSED BY BEFORE HIM, AND PROCLAIMED, THE LORD, THE LORD GOD, MERCIFUL AND GRACIOUS, LONG-SUFFERING, AND ABUNDANT IN GOODNESS AND TRUTH, KEEPING MERCY FOR THOUSANDS, FORGIVING INIQUITY AND TRANSGRESSION AND SIN, AND THAT WILL BY NO MEANS CLEAR THE GUILTY."—*Exod.* xxxiv. 6, 7.

HERE is the very voice of mercy from heaven to man, and mark, my soul, the gracious plenitude of truth. As if to assure or encourage timid and conscience-stricken man, we have attribute piled upon attribute, and the whole pointed out as a foundation of hope. Our hard thoughts of God are here at once rebuked and dispelled, and the chief of sinners may begin to rejoice. First, It is the Lord, the Lord God who speaks; but what is His name or His memorial among the sons of men? "He is merciful and gracious;" nay more, He is "long-suffering;" and further still, He is "abundant in goodness and in truth." But even more specific: He "keeps mercy for thousands, He forgives iniquity;" and as if that were not enough, we are farther assured that He also "forgives transgression and sin;" that is, every kind or degree of iniquity may be blotted out, according to the system which tells of the blood which cleanses from it all. May not the soul rejoice, then? Should it not exult in this mercy, and flee, in the full assurance of hope, to Him who is so mighty and so gracious to save?

Yet the mercy of God is not to encourage sin. Man's sin-loving soul would persuade him to continue in it, since grace so much abounds; but to cut off every pretext for that delusion, we read that the Lord, all-merciful as He is, will not, He cannot, "clear the guilty." And strange as it may sound, there never was a single sin committed which did not receive its due meed of punishment. Either in the sinner, or in the sinner's Substitute, every transgression of every shade and degree, must receive what it deserves. It may be pardoned to the sinner, but that is only because it was punished in the person of Him who died the Just for the unjust; and it is here that the believer sees at once the mercy of God expunging his sin, and the unswerving justice of Him who "will by no means clear," punishing that sin to the uttermost.

THE PROOF.

"To the Lord our God belong mercies and forgivenesses though we have rebelled against him."— DAN. ix. 9.

THE HYMN.

"O, mark the Just One's love to man!
The justice which arraigns
Is magnified by Christ the Lord,
And now our cause maintains."

The Wisdom of God.

"O THE DEPTHS OF THE RICHES BOTH OF THE WISDOM AND KNOWLEDGE OF GOD! HOW UNSEARCHABLE ARE HIS JUDGMENTS, AND HIS WAYS PAST FINDING OUT!"—*Rom.* xi. 33.

THIS is one of the depths of that ocean in which the humbled soul feels it would be lost, were not the everlasting arms underneath it and around it. The wisdom of God beams on the believer from the cross of Christ. But the Wonderful, the Counsellor, there appears in all his majesty, as well as in his wisdom; and the result is, assured confidence to the soul that believes. When such a man is enabled to draw near to the Holy One, under the shelter of the cross, sights are seen and utterances heard, by faith, in which he greatly exults One is taken and another left — behold the sovereignty of God: one reciprocates the love of God; another lives and dies at enmity with him: one rejoices in his mercy; another spurns it away: one admires and adores his wisdom; to another it is foolishness, and is rejected and despised: one feels the heart made glad by the beams of the Sun of Righteousness; another sees no beauty in Him, he continues blind, and even the wonder of Him who is the brightness of the Father's glory has no attractions for such a man. His foolish heart is darkened, and though the light of the knowledge of the glory of God be shining all around, all seems to him to be covered with a pall of darkness.

O my soul, hast thou been learning wisdom from Him in whom all its treasures are hid? Hast thou, in holy submission, laid thyself prostrate at the feet of Him of whom, and to whom, and through whom are all things? Then, being in a sinful creature's right position, enjoy the blessings provided by God our Saviour; cherish the wisdom which comes from above; and thus, as every thing which comes from heaven seeks back to its native home, the grace which has guided thee on the earth will lead thee to the house not made with hands eternal in the heavens. You have the first fruits here, the full harvest is on high; the grapes of Eshcol are tasted on earth, the vintage is all before you; the day of small things is now beheld, the eternal day is like the shining of seven suns.

THE PROOF.

"For of him and through him, and to him, are all things: to whom be glory for ever. Amen." — Rom. xi. 36.

THE HYMN.

"As tapers to the blazing sun,
  Or dew-drops to the mighty sea,
Are all the joys of earth and time
  To heaven's eternal ecstasy."

Hope in God.

"WHY ART THOU CAST DOWN, O MY SOUL? AND WHY ART THOU DISQUIETED WITHIN ME? HOPE THOU IN GOD: FOR I SHALL YET PRAISE HIM, WHO IS THE HEALTH OF MY COUNTENANCE AND MY GOD." — *Psalm* xlii. 11.

EVERY woe which man endures is designed to bring him nearer and nearer to his God, if he will be brought. Our spirit cleaves to the dust; sorrow comes to show us the folly of such a course. Man puts the creature in the Creator's place; tribulation shows him that the creature is a miserable comforter, and warns him, if he will be warned, to rest on the Almighty arm. Man is ever prone to seek that in sin which can be found only in holiness and God; but misery, perhaps acute and crushing, comes to show him that to be a sinner is to be wretched, whatever men may dream to the contrary. Now, under that discipline, a child of God gradually gathers wisdom; and one of his most resolute convictions is, that to his Father's arms he must flee for shelter in every hour of need. Is the soul burdened with a weight of sin? To his Father the believer flees, that the burden may be removed. Is it some relative woe that troubles him? That also he carries to God for comfort. Is he pained in spirit because the wicked are before him? Is his experience in some degree like that of the Saviour when he said: "O faithless and perverse generation, how long shall I be with you and suffer you?" That also the believer unbosoms to his God and Father. However cast down, however disquieted, he still hopes in God, and is not put to shame. He knows that the wood of a sweetening tree has been thrown into the bitter waters. He is well assured that all things are working together for good to them that love God. With God for his portion, what can such a man fear? With the Word of God as the foundation of his hope, can any measure of confidence be too sanguine? Nay, rather, O my soul, let me reason with thee, as David did with his. Is there not joy provided to soothe thee amid sorrow? or is there not One who says, in words of more than earthly tenderness, "As one whom his mother comforts, so will I comfort thee?"

THE PROOF.

"Although the fig tree shall not blossom, neither shall fruit be in the vines: the labour of the olive shall fail, and the fields shall yield no meat: the flock shall be cut off from the fold, and there shall be no herd in the stalls: Yet I will rejoice in the Lord, I will joy in the God of my salvation." — HAB. iii. 17, 18.

THE HYMN.

"The God of glory pours from heaven
His bounties on the sons of men;
And crowning all — the mind of God
Is imaged in man's soul again."

K

The Portion of the Soul.

"O MY GOD."—*Psalm* xl. 17.

SEPARATED as we are from God, not merely as creatures, but, moreover, as sinful creatures, one of the marvels of redemption is, that we can yet claim the Holy One as all our own. The man after God's own heart had learned habitually to do so, and upwards of two hundred times does he address God as his God, like one who knew that the Lord is the portion of his people. And O, is it not well that it is so? We try, indeed, to find a portion for the soul among the things which are seen and temporal. We laden ourselves with thick clay; we say to the gold, thou art my god, and to the fine gold, thou art my confidence; and amid that folly we dream that we are wise, although we are labouring in the fire. Chafed and disappointed on every side, we anticipate felicity in more, and more, and more of the creature — as if by enlarging our idols we could transmute them into the true God. But when the Spirit of God becomes our teacher, the living God becomes our portion. In him we live, and move, and have our being, and in him also we rejoice. Nearness to him is blessedness — the hiding of his countenance is woe. His condemnation we cannot brook; nay, the whole soul droops, and pines, and decays, unless we see light in God's light, and be made righteous with God's righteousness — and, as such, partakers of his peace.

Let the soul, then, delight itself in God: "Whom have I in heaven but thee? and there is none upon earth whom I can desire beside thee." "As the hart panteth after the waterbrooks, so panteth my soul after thee, O God. My soul thirsteth for God, the living God; when shall I come and appear before God?" Let these meditations of David be the meditations of our souls, and He who created the desire will gratify it. Our joy will be found in the smile of a reconciled God; and while others, wearied and worn out with a disappointing world, are greedily asking "Who will show us any good?" our souls will understand the prayer: "Lord, lift thou up the light of thy countenance upon us." The Spirit of adoption will then animate, and God in Christ become our all in all. *To be filled with all the fulness of God* — how gladdening, how satisfying, how surely is that the blessedness of heaven begun!

THE PROOF.

"For in him dwelleth all the fulness of the Godhead bodily." — Col. ii. 9.

THE HYMN.

"O blest exchange! for guilt and woe
My soul exults in hallowing grace;
God's Son to save — His Spirit to guide,
And fit me for his dwelling-place."

A Contrast.

"FOR MY THOUGHTS ARE NOT YOUR THOUGHTS, NEITHER ARE YOUR WAYS MY WAYS, SAITH THE LORD." — *Isaiah* lv. 8.

NO, O Lord, for thou bringest life out of death, and a grave is the scene of thy greatest triumph. Thou bringest glory, honor, and immortality there to light; and more than that, thou teachest the weak and the dying sons of men to exclaim, "O death, where is thy sting? O grave, where is thy victory?" To have abolished death, and bestowed on man, if he will receive the gift, a life which knows no death — that is proof enough that thy ways are not ours.

Or another — were another needed — is, that thou bringest countless blessings to man by means of the exhausted curse. Yea, he who was Jehovah's fellow was made a curse for us, that the wrath of an offended God might be rolled away, and all the honor of a violated law upheld; that mercy might flow forth to man, even while every sin is punished, and the guilty "by no means cleared."

And is it not another proof that thy thoughts are not ours, when it is to the ungodly that a Saviour is offered — for the unjust that the Just One died — that they are sinners, even the chief, whom the Redeemer sought to save? Had the thoughts of men been exercised upon a plan of salvation, or of escape from sin, it would certainly not have been for publicans and sinners that heaven would have been opened; but for those whom men regarded as virtuous, as good-hearted, or reformed. But "for sinners even the chief"—"yea, even for the rebellious also, that the Lord God might dwell among them"—behold the consummating proof that God's thoughts are not our thoughts, nor our ways his!

Yet his thoughts must become ours. We are to become like-minded with him — to will what he wills — to love what he loves — to shun what he prohibits. "This is the will of God, even our sanctification;" and, guided by that simple maxim, we are to go on unto perfection — we are to be perfect, even as our Father in heaven is perfect. Now, is that the aim of my soul? Is it thus like-minded with God? If it be, the Spirit is making all things new, and that soul, once disfigured and vile, is now on the way to the new Jerusalem.

THE PROOF.

"But God commendeth his love toward us, in that, while we were yet sinners, Christ died for us."— Rom. v. 8.

THE CONVICTION.

"The hand on the mouth, and the mouth in the dust
　Is the posture becoming in man;
When his proud heart would dare, by its glimmering light
　The ways of Jehovah to scan."

K *

The Man of Sorrows.

"AND JESUS SAID UNTO HIM, FOXES HAVE HOLES, AND BIRDS OF THE AIR HAVE NESTS; BUT THE SON OF MAN HATH NOT WHERE TO LAY HIS HEAD." — *Luke* IX. 58.

WHO uttered these pathetic words? Jesus, the Son of God, the Saviour of the sons of men; and as uttered by Him, do they not rank among the most remarkable of all the sentences that ever fell on mortal ear?

The beasts of the field have their cave, or their den, but the Son of God is a homeless wanderer on the earth which he made!

The birds of the air have nests constructed with rarest art, and with a view to perfect accommodation; but when they retired to these, there to repose for the night, the Son of God had to retire to the desert, there to weep, and agonize, and pray, till his locks were wet with the dews of heaven.

"By him were all things created that are in heaven, and that are in earth, visible and invisible, whether they be thrones or dominions, or principalities or powers, all things were created by him and for him; and he is over all things, and by him all things consist." And yet amid this mighty apparatus for promoting his glory, not a spot was found where the Holy One could repose. It was the monarch exiled by his rebel subjects — it was the beneficent parent banished by those over whom he was tenderly watching.

And why all this? Whence such abundant misery — such affluence of woe? It was that man might for ever rejoice. The tears and the agonies of the Saviour atoned for the sins of the saved. Did he wander over Palestine without a home? It was to secure for us an abode in the house of many mansions. Did he endure agony? did all forsake him and flee? It was that he might purchase for us the company of the just made perfect for ever. Was he a friendless and despised man? It was that "the love of God which passeth knowledge," might be unto all them that believe. Praise God, then, praise his holy name, at the remembrance of such mingled mercy, and love, and wisdom; and while the heart and soul are abased at the thought of a Saviour's agony, let them exult in his triumph; for it is his purpose that, through grace, all his ransomed should share it.

THE PROOF.

"To him that overcometh will I grant to sit with me in my throne, even as I also overcame, and am set down with my Father in his throne." — Rev. iii. 21.

THE HYMN.

"Who would not mourn? The Saviour dies,
　The thorn-crown round his brow.
Who would not joy? The Crucified
　Is throned in glory now."

The Blood of the Cross.

"IN CHRIST JESUS, YE WHO SOMETIMES WERE FAR OFF, ARE MADE NIGH BY THE BLOOD OF CHRIST."—*Eph.* ii. 13.

NOUGHT else could suffice whether for Jew or Gentile. Not the cattle on a thousand hills — not our children made to pass through the fire to some bloody Moloch — not our bodies given to be burned — not anguish on man's part like that of Juggernaut, nor the terrible penance of the superstition-stricken devotee. The exclusive, the divine method of reconciliation, is the blood of Christ shed on the cross, which guides us first to God's favor upon earth, and then to a crown of glory in the skies.

But how? What is the mighty virtue of that atonement? How does it make those nigh who were before afar off? It was written, "The soul that sinneth shall die." The Saviour died the substitute of his people, and so becomes their peace. It was written again, "Cursed is every one that continueth not in all the law." Man did not continue in it; but the Saviour kept it — he magnified it — he bore its curse — he exhausted its penalty — and so again he is our peace; we are made nigh by his blood. Alienated once, we are reconciled now. Enmity once, we are constrained by love now. Darkness once, we are now light in the Lord. Once far from God, and far from rightcousness, we are at length restored to our long-lost rank by Him who was man that He might endure, and God, that he might give infinite worth to his endurance.

Here, then, is the pillar and the ground of the believer's hope. Here he may rejoice with a portion of the joy which is unspeakable and full of glory. Being washed in the fountain open for sin, he is prepared to walk with God again in spirit and in truth; and while he sojourns, a pilgrim and a stranger here, his life is hid with Christ in God — his heart is in a better country, his Father's home on high.

THE PROOF.

"Now therefore ye are no more strangers and foreigners, but fellow-citizens with the saints, and of the household of God." — EPH. ii. 19.

THE HYMN.

"Trembling, weeping, dark, and sad —
  See the soul by Satan bound.
Hymns of praise most sweetly singing —
  See the soul which grace has found.

"Although a pilgrim here below,
  That saint is walking with his God,
Brought nigh to Him, nor grief nor joy
  Can tempt him from his loved abode."

The Mystery of Godliness.

"WITHOUT CONTROVERSY, GREAT IS THE MYSTERY OF GODLINESS."—1 *Tim.* iii. 16.

IT is fathomless — it is inscrutable — it prostrates proud but puny man in the dust. God was manifest in the flesh. The Word, by which all things were made — the Creator — was made flesh and dwelt among us. God in very deed dwelt among men on the earth, and there reflected the purities of heaven amid all that was polluting here below.

And O! mark what beatitudes are involved in this mystery of godliness!

By means of it, we can acquaint ourselves with God again; for he that has seen the Son hath seen the Father also, and that suffices.

By means of that mystery, an atonement becomes possible, for no creature could make reconciliation, and without shedding of blood there is no remission.

By means of that mystery, a righteousness is provided for the sinner, which even Jehovah can smile on, *for it is his own.*

By means of it, the gulf which separates the sinless Creator from the sinful creature is bridged over: all who will may now draw nigh, and walk with God as Enoch did.

Now, without recounting more, may not the soul re-echo the words which the Spirit taught the apostle to employ, "Without controversy, great is the mystery of godliness?" There the soul can find its God; and more than that, it can there prepare to be for ever with Him. Terror is all hushed now, for God is in Christ reconciling sinners to himself. Nothing greater than Jehovah can be thought of by man; nothing less could satisfy the cravings of his immortal and once god-like nature. Here, therefore, in the plenitude of Godhead as revealed in Christ, man finds the exhaustless fountain of his felicity, and having found it, he is ready to exclaim, "This is my rest, here I will stay, for I do like it." Is it so, my soul, with thee? Is this mystery of godliness thy exceeding joy? Then thou art Spirit-taught. Thou art one of those with whom He who is the mystery of godliness delights to dwell.

THE PROOF.

"No man knoweth . . . . . who the Father is but the Son, and he to whom the Son will reveal Him."—LUKE x. 22.

THE HYMN.

"Man's woe began when Satan dared
  God's image to efface;
Man's joy returns when Christ restores
  That image by his grace."

The Goodly Heritage.

"THE LORD IS MY PORTION, SAITH MY SOUL." — *Lam.* iii. 24.
"THE LORD'S PORTION IS HIS PEOPLE." — *Deut.* xxxii. 9.

THESE two related truths may well take rank among the wonders of redeeming love. "The Lord is the portion of his people." He does not leave them to feed upon vanity or ashes. It is not to the trifles of an hour, or even of an age, that they are abandoned. The Lord himself, the author of their being, and of all besides, is their enriching heritage.

And again, "The Lord's portion is his people." The love, the choice, is reciprocal. The redeemed are the peculiar heritage of Jehovah, as He is theirs. It is not in the worlds which he has created, or the glory of the firmament, whether we view it at midnight or mid-day; it is not in the richness and the luxuriance of earth, that the only wise God finds what advances his joy to the highest: it is in his redeemed, in those, namely, for whom the Saviour died, who have been sprinkled with atoning blood, and whom the Holy Spirit has renewed. Creation evinces God's power and Godhead, but the ransomed soul does more: it reflects the image of the Holy One, and is destined to an existence coeval with his own. Now, does my soul thus form an item in the portion of Jehovah? An

I counted among his heritage? In the day when he shall make up his jewels, will it appear that my immortal spirit ranks among them, and that my redemption is for ever to be deepening the bliss of the Most High? Then hosanna to the Son of David! Blessed is he who has come in the name of the Lord to save us! There is not a ransomed soul which may not now exclaim, "Surely the lines have fallen to us in pleasant places; we have gotten a goodly heritage"—as all my springs are in God, my redemption shall enhance the felicity of Godhead, world without end. The famished prodigal is the emblem of him who seeks some other portion. John reposing in the bosom of the Saviour is the representative of those whose minds are stayed on God.

THE PROOF.

"Know that the Lord hath set apart him that is godly for himself."—PSALM iv. 3.

"Whom have I in heaven but thee? and there is none upon earth that I desire besides thee."—PSALM lxxiii. 25.

THE HYMN.

"Could all the shining orbs on high,
  Or all the teeming wealth of earth,
  Fill up that void within the breast
  To which revolt from God gave birth?

"Nay, all the myriad worlds that roll
  Along the azure dome of Heaven,
  Would only mock the aching soul
  Till back the love of God be given."

L

The Boldness of Faith.

"HAVING BOLDNESS TO ENTER THE HOLIEST BY THE BLOOD OF JESUS." — *Heb.* x. 19.

TO be permitted to enter the holiest — the presence of God — at all, surely ranks among the highest of the privileges which man can enjoy. But to be permitted to enter with *boldness* — to come without slavish fear, but animated rather by the spirit of adoption, and confiding in the Holy God who cannot look on sin, constitutes one of the chief wonders of redeeming love, yet one in which the contrite soul may most assuredly rejoice. Nay more: the more boldness he displays, the more is God glorified. To come as if He grudged a pardon, as if He were reluctant to blot out iniquity, or to admit us into the Holiest, is to grieve his Spirit, or undervalue his love. But to come perfectly abased as to ourselves, yet confiding in the finished work of Christ, and understanding that God is more glorified in forgiving through him, than in condemning our race had no Mediator appeared — that is the right evangelical ground, and the right evangelical spirit. As long as I think that salvation in any degree depends on me, I cannot but come before God with fear and trembling. But when I see that the work was finished in the divine counsels before the world began, and actually accomplished at Jerusalem in the fulness of time, then the spirit of bondage disappears. The soul glories now in the Lord; God is honored, and man is at once exalted and abased — abased as a sinner, exalted as one to whose conscience that blood which cleanses from all sin has been applied.

And how is the case with my soul? Let every one who would deal faithfully regarding his eternal concerns solemnly say, Have I learned to come boldly through the blood of Jesus? Then my religion is the religion which God has revealed, which came from heaven and which guides us to it. But do I still come haunted by fear, as if God would not hear and answer, *even for Christ's sake?* Then my religion is not yet God's; I need the unction of the Holy One to show me the liberty which the Son of God imparts.

THE PROOF.

"Stand fast therefore in the liberty wherewith Christ hath made us free, and be not entangled again with the yoke of bondage." — GAL. v. 1.

THE HYMN.

"As morning lifts her dewy veil
To smile on earth and sea,
So heavenly love illumines man —
Would that it beamed on me!

"But why should doubt becloud the **mind**?
Why trembling seek our God?
Has Christ not died? Is peace not **made**
By His atoning blood?"

The True Ambition.

"WHO CAN BRING A CLEAN THING OUT OF AN UNCLEAN? NOT ONE." — *Job* xiv. 4.

AND yet that must be done ere man can have solid hope. It is not enough that sin be cancelled. Merely to blot my iniquities from the book of God's remembrance, would not make me fit for heaven. The pure must supplant the polluted, ere the soul can be prepared for glory, and the society of the just made perfect. It is the sure decree of God, that nothing that defiles, nothing that loves or makes a lie, can ever stand before him; and the first act of faith, therefore, is to lead us to the fountain opened for sin, to sprinkle us with the blood which cleanses from it all. Transformed by that new-creating Spirit, whose work and glory it is to make the Ethiopian change his skin and the leopard his spots, we start on that career which ends where eternity is our existence, and the Eternal our portion.

And from the moment that that work is begun, it advances and grows till we reach the stature of perfection. We cannot but grow in grace. Instead of comparing ourselves among ourselves, the divine Standard becomes our rule, and our life-long aim is to press nearer and nearer to it. If, then, that be my aim — if I am seeking to go on unto perfection, to **grow** in grace, to wash my hands in innocency, and hate every false way — if I am learning to endure no wicked thing before me, but evermore to seek to be more holy, more humble, more Christ-like, then may hope be cherished for such a soul; it may begin to sing in the good way of the Lord: that holiness without which no man shall see Him is apparent, and He who has begun the good work will carry it on to completion: He will present that soul to himself at last, without spot or wrinkle or any such thing. The Saviour will eternally behold in it the travail of his soul, while it will eternally behold in the Saviour the chief among ten thousand, and altogether lovely. To aim at that is the true ambition, while that soul is contented to grovel in the dust which has not learned "earnestly to covet that best gift."

THE PROOF.

"**And** that ye put on the new man, which after God is created **in righteousness** and true holiness." — EPHES. iv. 24.

THE HYMN.

" Upward, my heart!
  Thy Saviour smiles;
 Haste, seek his grace,
  What snare beguiles?

" Covet his glory,
  Welcome his peace,
 Cherish his Spirit —
  Then bondage will cease."

Strength in Weakness.

"WHEN I AM WEAK, THEN AM I STRONG. — 2 *Cor.* xii. 10.

SUCH is the experience of every child of God — weak in himself, but strong in the Lord, unstable as water, and unable to excel, yet able to do all things through Jesus Christ who strengthens him. And let the earnest soul rejoice that it is not our strength that Jehovah requires, for our strength is his rival. It is our weakness, and that is his glorifier: His strength is made perfect thereby, and so his ransomed rejoice.

Here, then, is the secret of the believer's strength — to lay hold of the right arm which wields the world. Is that believer compassed about with sorrow? Is his heart sinking within him, under some pressing or some dreaded calamity? Is it old age, with its heavy burden and its frequent friendlessness? Is it poverty, with its long train of woes? Is it the crushing burden of sin? Is it coming death, and after death the judgment? Whatever it may be, the believer's strength is found in clinging to the right arm of the redeemer's righteousness. He should cast his burden on the Lord, who can bear the weakest up under the pressure of six troubles, yea of seven. It is thus that we learn why Paul gloried in infirmities; thus that we feel we are made more than conquerors, and thus that we learn to admire the loving-kindness of the Lord in upholding the weak, investing them with his own omnipotence as a shield, or defending them from extinction like a spark in the ocean. And O do not forget the mysterious might of the Saviour's weakness, who conquered death, and triumphed over the grave, while they seemed to rush on to destroy him. It was by submission that he vanquished, and in his strength the worm Jacob will do the same. "Thy strength is to sit still." "Be still and know that I am God" is a fountain at once of strength to the weak, and of peace to the troubled.

THE PROOF.

"Fear not, thou worm Jacob, and ye men of Israel; I will help thee, saith the Lord, and thy Redeemer, the Holy One of Israel."—Isaiah xli. 14.

THE TRIUMPH.

"Poor, and yet rich, God's holy ones
  Are by the world unknown;
When hated, love repays the ill —
  They know that He will own.

"Cast down, but not forsaken;
  Oppressed, yet gladdened still
Reviled by man, and blest by God,
  They welcome all His will."

The Stay of the Saint.

"THEIR STRENGTH IS TO SIT STILL." — *Isaiah* xxx 7.

VAIN is the help of man. To go to Egypt or Assyria for help — that is, to the Lord's enemies for strength to fight his battles — is to sin against the Holy One. When troubles come and danger lowers, far better to be still, and know that He is God, than to trust in princes or men's sons, in whom there is no stay.

Is sin assailing us with some strong temptation, and threatening to sweep every good thing in the soul before it? Then stand still, my soul, but stand in faith, and thou shalt see the salvation of our God.

Or have the effects of sin come upon us like a flood? Are we like the Hebrews of old at Pi-hahiroth, when the rocks hemmed them in on either side, while Pharaoh was behind, and the Red Sea before? Still a believer's strength is to sit still: if he sit still in faith, God will work, and none shall hinder. The extremity of his people is the time for Him to rise and show that He is God indeed — even their God, to rescue and shield.

Or is the aged pilgrim near the close of his journey? Does he see the vista of this weary life closed by an open grave — the portals of eternity? Then also man's strength is to sit still, for "they that wait upon the Lord shall renew their strength; they shall mount up on wings as eagles; they shall run and not be weary; they shall walk and not faint." Wait on the Lord, then; be of good courage, and he shall strengthen thine heart: wait, I say, upon the Lord. In patience possess your soul, and all that can impede a believer's heavenward progress will either be taken out of the way, or made to minister to his progress. As burnishing brightens steel, and the crucible tests the gold, so trials and temptations teach the child of God where his strength is found.

THE PROOF.

"Be still, and know that I am God: I will be exalted among the heathen, I will be exalted in the earth."— PSALM xlvi. 10.

THE HYMN.

"Like the palm trees of Elim to Israel of old,
  The Lord is our shelter and rest;
And the soul that is canopied under his love
  May taste of the joys of the blest.

"Have sin and its follies still power to seduce?
  Then our portion can only be woe;
But, strong in his grace, are we armed for the fight?
  Then, hosanna! we vanquish the foe."

The Spirit of Holiness.

"KNOW YE NOT THAT YE ARE THE TEMPLE OF GOD, AND THAT THE SPIRIT OF GOD DWELLETH IN YOU." — 1 *Cor.* iii. 16

SUCH honor have all God's saints, and this indwelling of the Spirit is surely to be ranked among the highest privileges which the ransomed of the Lord enjoy on earth.

But, O my soul, let it lay thee in the dust to notice the results which flow from this privilege; and beware lest thou approach the sin against the Holy Ghost, and earn the woe pronounced on Chorazin, Bethsaida, and Capernaum. Is indwelling sin struggling for the mastery? The more on that account honor the indwelling Spirit. Is temptation assailing? Then reinforce thy purpose to resist it, by recollecting that thou art a temple of the Holy Ghost; that He dwells in thee, and seeks to spread a purity like that of heaven throughout all the functions of the inner man. Or hast thou sinned? Dost thou call to mind the transgressions of thy youth, and art then compelled to sit in the dust, and mourn in thy complaint, because of "the abominable thing?" Then, O let it deepen thy shame, and call forth a profounder penitence, to remember that that sin was committed under the very eye of the Author of holiness; that it was done in spite of his strivings; that He was grieved whilst thou wert sinning; and if he is not quenched, it is because he is God and not man.

Yet be encouraged also. That very Spirit is the Spirit of love. It is he that sprinkles us with the blood which cleanses, and if the consciousness of sin urge thee nearer to the fountain, the God of pardons will be glorified there: thou shalt be abased, and holy circumspection against future sin promoted. It is thus that the Holy One makes the wrath of man to praise him, and thus that the remembrance of our sins in the past is overruled to promote our circumspection for the future. And if it be thus with sinners in general, surely it should happen most of all with those who rank among "the chief." To have sinned against grace, against light, against privilege, and countless mercies, may well teach us to walk humbly with our God, and often to exclaim, "O to grace how great a debtor!"

THE PROOF.

"Wherefore I say unto you, All manner of sin and blasphemy shall be forgiven unto men: but the blasphemy against the Holy Ghost shall not be forgiven unto men."—MATT. xii. 31.

THE HYMN.

"Like some fair flower from sunny climes,
   Nipt by the northern blast,
Grace pines and droops whene'er the Sun
   Of souls is overcast.

"But does the Spirit screen the germ?
   Do heavenly dews descend?
Then like the gales of Araby,
   These dews sweet odors send."

The True Forgiveness.

"THERE IS FORGIVENESS WITH THEE THAT THOU MAYST BE FEARED."—*Psalm* cxxx. 4.

THERE is no discovery more rare than that God is a God of mercy. All men think, indeed, that they believe it, but they are only believing a delusion. They believe that a being whom they *call* God is merciful; but that God is a creature of their own fancy—easy, indulgent, and, in truth, not holy—not the God who "will by no means clear the guilty." And when men are undeceived, when the Spirit of truth has showed them the true character of God, as a just God and an holy, men who were formerly full of hope speedily begin to despair. Some who formerly supposed that they were reposing on the mercy of God, discover that they were only trying to hide from Him in some refuge of lies; and of all the attempts which man can make, the most difficult is to convince an awakened sinner that God will have mercy *upon him*. Even the word of the Faithful and the True Witness does not assure such a soul.

And never till men see the glory of God in the face of Jesus Christ, do they believe in his pardoning mercy; nor till they see how Christ died, the just for the unjust, can they hope in their God. Before that, they may presume—only after it can they honor and confide in Him whose tender mercies are over all His other works, in Jesus Christ our Lord.

Now, is it on God's covenant mercy that my soul is reposing, or on some delusive figment, the phantom mercy of a fictitious God? There *is* forgiveness with God: He delights to pardon, and a thousand passages prove it; but it is pardon in a peculiar way — through the Mediator of the eternal covenant, or not at all. Hope thou in *that*, and God will be feared; but hope in aught besides, and that hope will be quenched in despair. And O how blessed is the soul when it is taught by the Spirit to believe that its transgression is forgiven, that its sin is covered, and that the Lord imputes no iniquity! The kingdom of God is then set up within us, and guided by the wisdom which comes from above, we shall dwell at last and for ever upon God's holy mountain.

THE PROOF.

"Hide thy face from my sins, and blot out all mine iniquities." — Psalm li. 9.

THE HYMN.

"With faith to save, and Love to warm,
  And Hope to light our way,
The skyward path we tread with joy,
  Our God our strength and stay.

"The pilgrim's staff we all must grasp,
  The warrior's shield must bear;
But nerved by grace, the pardoned soul
  Each spiritual foe can dare."

The Believer Complete.

"YE ARE COMPLETE IN HIM."—*Col.* ii. 10.

COMPLETE for acceptance with God, and justification before Him; for we are made the righteousness of God in Christ.

— Complete for competing with all the ills of life though they may, in God's holy providence, come rolling in like wave upon wave in a troubled sea.

— Complete for resisting all the assaults of indwelling sin within, and temptation from without, if we rest on the grace provided, or the strength which is almighty.

Not complete in holiness yet, but complete in all that is needed to help us to perfect holiness in the fear of the Lord.

— Complete for meeting God in judgment, if we will consent to plead the finished work, the perfect righteousness of the Son of God, the Saviour of the sons of men. Poor, and wretched, and miserable, and naked in ourselves, we may yet be accepted in the Beloved; according to the mind of God, we are to be presented unto Him at last without spot, or wrinkle, or any such thing.

"*Complete in Christ,*" then — be that the sheet-anchor, the refuge, the asylum of the soul. Never can the Holy One justify or sanction what is incomplete; and my reason and my conscience tell me, that if He were to justify what is imperfect, He would himself become imperfect also. But let all that is within me bless God's holy name: He healeth *all* our diseases; He cleanses us from *all* our iniquity; He redeems Israel from *all* his transgressions; and though the believer, when thus visited in mercy, may be deeply abased at the remembrance of his sins, yet looking unto Jesus, he can through him look unto God and hope.

But the question recurs to the anxious soul — How may *I* be made complete? My iniquities have gone over my head; they have cried to the justice of God for punishment; how then can I be complete? The answer is, "All things are possible, only believe." Let faith rest upon the Saviour of the lost, and then, by the appointment of God we are righteous with the Saviour's righteousness; we are strong in the Saviour's strength, and preparing for the Saviour's heaven.

THE PROOF.

"To the praise of the glory of his grace, wherein he hath made us accepted in the Beloved." — EPH. i. 6.

THE HYMN.

"Polluted man would climb to heaven,
 And claim a welcome there;
But ransomed souls, 'complete in **Christ**,'
 Alone its joys can share."

The Right Way.

"HE LED THEM FORTH BY THE RIGHT WAY, THAT THEY MIGHT GO TO A CITY OF HABITATION." — *Psalm* cvii. 7.

IT was not the most direct path by which the Hebrews were led from Egypt to Canaan. Nay, there were countless windings in it. For their waywardness they had often to retrace their steps; and after weeks, or months, or years of weary wandering, you might find them farther from the land of promise than when that period began. But in so far as their Lord and King was leading, it was still the right way —

— It was the right way to humble them and reprove their waywardness.

It was the right way to show that it was not for their sakes that the Lord chose the Hebrews as a people to himself.

It was the right way to wean them from self-confidence.

It was the right way to train them for the land of promise.

And it was the right way to make their wanderings in the desert a model for the believer's wanderings through this world to a better.

Now, has my soul seen the wisdom of God in thus leading the Hebrews? Is it plain that in very faithfulness he afflicted them, and that even when the fiery serpents came, or when the earth opened for the guilty, it was all to unveil the character of Jehovah as "the Just God and the Holy?"

If these discoveries be made, let the soul which has made them rejoice: the pillar of cloud and of fire which guided the Hebrews of old, will conduct it to glory. And O, let it never be forgotten by whose power rough places in the desert are still made smooth, and high places still made level. Had some one become a pauper to enrich us, what should be our feelings towards him? If some one had gone into exile, that we might be free to return to our father's home, what should be our gratitude? If some one had submitted to degradation and death, that we might be exa'ed, how should we respond to that interposition? Now, in all these ways, the Shepherd of Israel has acted towards those whom he is guiding. How strange, then, how infatuated they who refuse even to be guided in the right way to the city of our God!

THE PROOF.

"Therefore, behold, I will allure her, and bring her into the wilderness, and speak comfortably unto her."— Hosea ii. 14.

THE HYMN.

"In exile from his native heaven,
  The lowly Saviour dwelt—
 O why his tears, his woes, his tomb?
  He bore his people's guilt."

The Glory of Man.

"PARTAKERS OF THE DIVINE NATURE."—2 *Peter* i. 4.

THIS seems the consummation of religion. It is paradise renewed, for it is God restored to man, and man to God. It is the soul at rest, sanctified, and serenely blessed, whatever be the trials of its earthly lot.

It is true, many have perverted this doctrine, as if man were to be absorbed into Godhead, as rivers are lost in the ocean, or drops in the river. "Souls lose their unity," said a mystic, "and in that loss become *one* with God;" and "there are graces by which the souls which possess them become *truly gods*, by being made partakers of the Divine nature." But these are wild exaggerations, or perversions of the truth. According to it, we love as God loves; we shun what God forbids; we pursue what he appoints, when our nature has been renewed. Being made one spirit with the Lord, we are like-minded with him; but to speak of partaking of the essence of Godhead, is either blasphemy on the one hand, or pantheism on the other. Not fused into the Divine essence, but holy, for God is holy; yea, "perfect even as our Father in heaven is perfect"—behold the supreme and the true ambition of man, the true meaning of our being partakers of the Divine nature, through his promises of truth. Rejoice, then, O my soul, that it is thy destiny in Christ, to wear God's image as Adam wore it at the first. It may be with thee as with him who said —

> "O let my heart, by fatal absence rent,
> Feel what I sing, and bleed while I lament;
> Who roams in exile from his parent bower,
> Pants to return, and chides each lingering hour."

But all will end in blessedness at last, when the ransomed shall be for ever with the Lord; when they shall follow the Lamb whithersoever he leads, and literally and for ever live, and move, and have their being in God. The religion which the Spirit of God plants by his omnipotent grace in the heart, would not have been complete had it stopped short of restoring God to man. That is the universal want of fallen human nature; be that want supplied, and " that sufficeth."

THE PROOF.

"He that is joined unto the Lord is one spirit" — 1 Cor. vi. 17.

THE HYMN.

> "An aching void within the troubled breast;
> A dreary doom which baffles mortal power;
> Woe piled on woe, no spot whereon to rest;
> Behind, remorse — before, dark terrors lower; —

> " Behold the picture of man's guilty state,
> When Retribution, urged by Conscience, wakes:
> Yet, 'GOD WITH US' sheds hope upon the soul;
> For Grace can rescue him that sadly quakes."

The Truth Imperishable.

"BEHOLD, THE BUSH BURNED WITH FIRE, AND THE BUSH WAS NOT CONSUMED." — *Exod.* iii. 2.

AN emblem this of God's holy truth in the world, and in the soul. The empire of the Redeemer, and its continued existence, are marvels upon earth. Assailed, corrupted, denied, or perverted on every side, it still survives. The Spirit of life is its omnipotent defender, and were that not the case, it would be swept from the face of the earth. Its existence is not merely threatened: it is an anomaly — it is hidden, and cannot be discerned; but, as far as it is known, it is offensive to millions. Yet still, amid all that is anomalous, or all that is mysterious and unearthly there, "the bush is not consumed." Fear not, then — the Zionward soul may exclaim — He whose word called the universe into being, and whose will gives it law, is thy sure defence. His eye is ever on the truth. It may seem as if the little spark could be easily extinguished, or the wasted body soon worn down, or the tempted soul soon overcome, or the truth which is like a grain of mustard seed easily crushed; but *Omnipotence prevents it.* That truth once planted in the soul, is indestructible like its Author. The little spark once kindled, can never be extinguished. The soul once renewed, is renewed for ever.

"How happy we live if *a shadow* could last!" may well be the exclamation of the worldly; but, "I am persuaded that God can keep what I have committed to his care," may be the response of the believing soul. And as I pass onward in my pilgrimage, I feel all these things more deeply gladdening. Friends die, but the Lord liveth; the body decays, but the soul is renewed day by day. I find greater sweetness in the word, and greater firmness in faith, through the unction of the Holy One, as years pass away; and though I feel that a single hour of self-reliance would ruin all, I can exult in the thought that "None can pluck us out of our Father's hand."

THE PROOF.

"For I am persuaded, that neither death, nor life, nor angels, nor principalities, nor powers, nor things present, nor things to come, nor height, nor depth, nor any other creature, shall be able to separate us from the love of God, which is in Christ Jesus, our Lord." — Rom. viii. 38, 39.

THE HYMN.

"The firmest friends may change,
  The best beloved may leave us,
Familiar ones grow strange,
  Or death of all bereave us.

"Where is the love undying?
  The friend who never fails?
On whom the heart relying
  May trust when grief assails?

"Behold the Lamb who beareth
  Believers' sins away:
For such he ever careth —
  And now — as yesterday."

The Heavenly Witness.

"THE SPIRIT ITSELF BEARETH WITNESS WITH OUR SPIRIT, THAT WE ARE THE CHILDREN OF GOD." — *Rom.* viii. 16.

THE more we ponder on the Word of God, the more profound do its lessons appear, and the loftier the privileges prepared for the children of God. Though "it doth not yet appear what we shall be," there are joys imparted and blessings made sure, such as may plant the believer on the threshold of heaven. How marvellous, for example, that the Spirit of God should dwell in the soul, and testify to the believer regarding his character and prospects! First, that blessed visitant comes to convince us of sin; then he converts us from it; then he leads us into all truth — he shows us the things which are Christ's; amid all our waywardness, he makes us "holiness to the Lord;" and by applying the truth to the soul, by enabling us to feel its power, and live under its influence, he gradually produces the conviction, more or less strong according to the simplicity of our faith, that we are the children of God. He sheds light upon the holy page. He sheds light also upon our darkened minds; and when the truth is thus stamped upon them, the result is the conviction that we are born of God — that we are renewed in the spirit of our mind. In other words, holiness is the result, and as holiness, or Christ-likeness, is the family characteristic of the children of God, the soul, thus guided by the Spirit, grows assured that nothing can separate it from the love of God which is in Christ Jesus. And surely every rational and self-loving man should covet earnestly this best gift, the proof and evidence of every other. Can he be rational in any saving sense, who grieves this Spirit, and so obliterates by his own hand every possible trace that he is born of God? O man of God, flee these things. Remember that grieving the Holy Spirit of promise, is on the way to quenching Him, and quenching Him is the unpardonable sin. Every alternative has failed, and hope is for ever gone, when man is so mature in guilt that he is let alone by the Spirit to sin with a high hand, and yet without compunction or alarm.

THE PROOF.

"Teach me to do thy will; for thou art my God; thy Spirit is good; lead me into the land of uprightness." — PSALM cxliii. 10.

THE HYMN.

"Would mortals know the power of truth
    Pure as it comes from heaven?
Or taste its sweetness to the soul
    Which feels it is forgiven?

"The Spirit comes — then truth is sweet
    As odours shed at eve;
And bright as are the radiant beams
    When first yon orb they leave."

The Comprehensive Prayer.

"I BESEECH THEE, SHOW ME THY GLORY." — *Exod.* xxxiii. 18

THY glory in Creation is transcendent! The first question which it suggests baffles my power — How was all this summoned into being out of nothing? I am silent, and adore, for I cannot comprehend.

Thy glory in Providence is ineffable. From the sand-grain to the globe — from an atom to unnumbered worlds — all is under thy control. Every movement thou dost regulate. Every want thou dost supply. "The eyes of all things wait on thee." "Not a sparrow falls to the ground without our heavenly Father."

But thy glory in Redemption transcends all these. Show me *that* glory — the glory which beamed in him who is the express image of thy person. O answer the prayer, and show me "the light of the knowledge of thy glory in the face of Jesus Christ!"

— The glory of thy justice, untarnished even while thou passest by the transgressions of thy people, or while thou savest even the ungodly.

— The glory of thy mercy, rejoicing over judgment, and not willing that any should perish — nay, blotting out iniquity, and not remembering transgression.

—The glory of thy love, when thou didst give up thy Son to die that man might live.

—The glory of thy long-suffering in bearing with the wayward amid ten thousand sins.

—The glory of thy power, in making even me more than a conqueror.

—The glory of thy faithfulness, in completing the work which thou hast begun, and guiding many sons and daughters to glory. Through Him who is the Head of the whole creation, the image of the invisible God, enlighten my darkened soul. While I am yet speaking, do thou hear; and O grant that I may be transformed into thine image, from glory to glory, as by the Spirit of the Lord. At the contemplation of all this, my soul, conscious as it is of guilt, shrinks back, as if it were baseless presumption in me to hope that this should be my portion. But is it not upon thine own truth that we repose? In that also thy glory is displayed; and reposing there, the soul grows strong — it enjoys in foretaste the glory of the ransomed.

THE PROOF.

"For God, who commanded the light to shine out of darkness hath shined in our hearts, to give the light of the knowledge of the glory of God in the face of Jesus Christ." — 2 Cor. iv. 6.

THE HYMN.

"God's glory beams once more on man —
  No phantom bliss His love bestows;
 In Christ we see the Father shine,
  And hail the source whence glory flows."

The Obedience of One.

"BY THE OBEDIENCE OF ONE, SHALL MANY BE MADE RIGHTEOUS." — *Rom.* v. 19.

THIS is the key-note of the Gospel; upon this every thing depends. The law was magnified by one, even by its Author. Every jot and tittle was upheld. All its penalty was exhausted, and by the death of "one" for "many," the curse was averted — the woe which it entailed was rolled away: so that in that respect, as well as many others, the believer in Jesus can now rejoice in the liberty which he imparts.

But how made righteous? By the decision of the Judge himself. The righteousness of the "One," received by faith in terms of the divine appointment, covers each soul of the "many;" and clothed therewith, every believing one is pardoned and accepted — is righteous with the righteousness of God — and obtains an inheritance among the ransomed for ever.

And what exactly is the province of faith in this transaction? Simply to receive what God offers; it is the hand which takes and keeps hold of the gift. It is not a work. It has no merit. It merely welcomes what God in mercy confers. So far from possessing any intrinsic power, it is the peculiar **province** of faith to take man out of himself, as poor, and needy, and helpless, that he may receive and rest upon another. Faith, moreover, is a gift of God; so that in every sense, its office is to denude the creature, and teach him to glory only in the Lord. And surely there can be nothing more glorifying to God, or gladdening to man, than to be "made righteous" on terms so simple, so godlike, and so perfect? Is it not our reasonable service to dedicate ourselves, souls and bodies, living sacrifices to Him, who provided, and who offered the gift which thus justifies and saves, and places us in the vestibule of heaven?

THE PROOF.

"Whom God hath set forth . . . . to declare . . . . his righteousness; that He might be just, and the justifier of him that believeth in Jesus." — ROM. iii. 25, 26.

THE HYMN.

"With bloody rites the heathen try
    To turn away their idols' ire:
But glory to our God on high!
    Christ's woes at once our hopes inspire.

"With hearts, and thoughts, and deeds impure,
    Sin-blinded men would meet their God;
And claim for their eternal home,
    His stainless and serene abode.

"But, O my soul, repose alone
    Upon the Rock in Zion laid,
Thy only plea — Christ's finished work,
    Thy hope — the great atonement made."

The Message of Peace.

"IF WE CONFESS OUR SINS, HE IS FAITHFUL AND JUST TO FORGIVE US OUR SINS, AND TO CLEANSE US FROM ALL UNRIGHTEOUSNESS."—1 *John* i. 9.

THIS is one of the most wonderful of all the sayings which embody the gospel of the grace of God. That the Holy One should be just to punish, we can easily understand, but that he should be just to pardon, just to be merciful, just to save the sinner from self-ruin, and self-inflicted everlasting woe; *that* ranks among the most marvellous of the divine disclosures.

And yet such is the basis laid for the sinner's joy and consolation, when that sinner becomes a believer; the very attribute which frowns in terrible majesty on the guilty soul becomes the guaranty of that believer. Justice, satisfied by a divine Substitute and Surety, ceases to demand the sinner's condemnation; nay, it proclaims that there is no condemnation for them that believe; it enforces these glad tidings by the assurance that God is faithful and just to forgive; his word is pledged; his favor is made sure by two immutable things, God's unchanging truth, and God's untarnishable justice: The trembling transgressor may have good hope through grace, when he flees like a prisoner of hope to the stronghold of the gospel — the city of refuge for the soul.

While we gaze on those wondrous galvanic wires which now line certain of our great highways, it is possible that there may be rushing along them some message of deep and startling import. They may be charged with death to some criminal who is about to be arrested; or with freedom to some prisoner who is to be released. It may be a message which shall plunge one family into woe, or elevate another to a pinnacle of happiness; but merely by gazing we cannot read the message. And so, while man is pondering the question, How will God deal with sinners? we cannot, cannot answer it, as long as we have only reason or conscience to guide us. But open the book of God; hear the Divine mind; and there He speaks peace to his people. He bids us delight in the abundance of peace; and the very fountain-head of that felicity is, that God is "faithful and just to forgive."

THE PROOF.

"Peace, peace to him that is afar off, and to him that is near, saith the Lord; and I will heal him."—Isaiah lvii. 19.

THE HYMN.

" The flaming sword of Cherubims
   Drove guilty man from Eden's bowers;
But now that sword in mercy gleams
   To point the way to Salem's towers."

Adoption.

"BEHOLD, WHAT MANNER OF LOVE THE FATHER HATH BESTOWED UPON US, THAT WE SHOULD BE CALLED THE SONS OF GOD." — 1 *John* iii. 1.

LIGHTNING is ever the brightest when it is seen playing on the bosom of a dark thunder-cloud; and the love of God appears most conspicuous when seen against the dark background of man's enmity against him. It was with some such feeling of contrast that John exclaimed, "Behold what manner of love the Father hath bestowed upon us!" It was not ordinary love, or love in ordinary circumstances — it was love to creatures in a state of rebellion. It was not love to those who were suing for mercy, or soliciting favor; but to creatures whose hearts were stout against their God. Or it was not such love as would merely rank us among the hired servants; it made us sons, the very sons of God. The Spirit of his Son was shed abroad in our hearts — we could thus call our God our Father. Through the first-born of many brethren, we were made members of the family of the redeemed, and in Him we acquired a right to all the privileges of children. No more aliens, or strangers. No more enemies, or rebels. No more fighting against God. Nay, we repose upon his love; and borne up thereby, the soul of the believer, though humbled to the dust by the loving-kindness of the Lord, can yet anticipate the existence where faith shall cease, for it will have done its work; and hope shall be over, for fruition will have taken its place; and love — the love of God to the redeemed, and of the redeemed to God — shall be paramount in the New Jerusalem — the home of the blessed who have been cleansed in atoning blood. Is that thy portion, O my soul?

Amid all the blessings which redeeming blood has secured for man, there is none more precious than this. In prayer, how harassing to come as a slave, dreading rejection and repulse! but how soothing to approach the throne as children approaching a father, assured of a welcome, and of blessings beyond what mortal eye has seen! That is the spirit which all should cherish; and were it cherished as it ought to be, the complaint of old, "If I be a father, where is mine honor?" would cease for ever.

THE PROOF.

"Because ye are sons, God hath sent forth the Spirit of his Son into your hearts, crying, Abba, Father." — GAL. iv. 6.

THE HYMN.

"See that fond parent share her crust
    With those around her heart entwined;
Mark how she screens from every blast
    That babe upon her breast reclined.

"And shall a heavenly Father less
    Regard the objects of his care?
Nay, mortal love but echoes His —
    Even prodigals his pity share."

The Saviour's Humiliation.

"I AM A WORM, AND NO MAN." — *Psalm* xxii. 6.

HOW surely He to whom these words apply is the "Wonderful!" What a paradox his whole character appears to the eye of man! The brightness of the Father's glory, yet without a home on earth! The image of the invisible God, yet rejected and despised of men! The mystery of godliness, yet marred more than any man! The adored of angels, and yet the crucified of sinners! God our Saviour — Jehovah our Righteousness — God with us; and yet, according to his own language, "a worm and no man; a reproach of men, and despised of the people!"

Divine wisdom can harmonize these two. The wisdom which the Holy Spirit teaches can enable us, not merely to comprehend, but to exult in the apparently conflicting truths: Man to endure; God to give value to endurance, which needed to be infinite: Man to keep the law; and God to give grandeur to that obedience, that the law might be magnified and made honorable: Man to die; and God to make that death adequate to the mighty work of reconciliation and purity, which it was designed to advance; — that is the solution of the problem, the explanation of the paradox. But, O my soul, turning from the paradox, cling to the results of the Redeemer's humiliation. See him in his agony! that was for thee, if thou believe upon his name. Behold him despised and outcast — that was for thee! And in the grave — that was for thee! But behold him also on the throne — He is there for thee! and more than that, He will place thee there beside him. By holiness, then, of heart, speech, and behavior, prepare to be for ever with the Lord. O banish pride, when the Saviour was so lowly. Be much in the dust, seeing that he stooped even to the grave. He that would be great must begin by being little; and the greatest soul is not that which can explain the theory of the world, or harmonize and control the interests of nations, but that which is most lowly, meek, and Christlike.

THE PROOF.

"In the beginning was the Word, and the Word was with God, and the Word was God." — JOHN i. 1.

THE HYMN.

"O, gaze into that open grave;
 The Saviour once was there!
Then haste, entomb each thought of pride,
 And thus for life prepare."

Joy in God.

"WE JOY IN GOD, THROUGH OUR LORD JESUS CHRIST, BY WHOM WE HAVE NOW RECEIVED THE ATONEMENT." — *Rom.* v. 11.

WITHOUT an atonement we could never have joyed in God, for without shedding of blood there is no remission; and if there be no remission, there is no peace, or no communion with God, except that of the criminal with the judge. But when we repose on the atonement, and are thereby reconciled unto God, then begins our joy, for sin is taken away. Its guilt is cancelled; its pollution is supplanted by purity; its condemning power is encountered for us, and turned aside. God now becomes our chief good and chief joy. The soul reposes upon him. It delights to be near him. Communion with him gladdens the believer, and when that communion is withheld, he can enter, in some measure, into the deep words, "My God, my God, why hast thou forsaken me!" In short, the favor of God, as a covenant God in Christ, prompts man to sing in the house of his pilgrimage; he can endure even a great fight of afflictions, if the light of God's countenance be shining upon him.

Is it the case, then, that I thus joy in God? Am I still like Adam when he fled to hide from Him amid the trees of the garden, because conscience accuses; or have I been brought nigh by the blood of the cross? Is it the case that I still regard the service of God a weariness and a bondage; or do I delight in drawing near to Him as my Father who is in heaven? His house, his people, his word, his day — are all these honored, loved, and revered by me for his sake; or is his house shunned, or rarely frequented? Are his people the men of my counsel; or are they disliked and avoided? Is his word sweet to my taste, like honey from the comb; or do I prefer every book to God's? Do I reckon his day the honorable of the Lord, and do I honor it? Then the grace which came by Jesus Christ has touched the heart; and, savoring the things which be of God on earth, the house not made with hands, eternal in the heavens, will be the soul's abode for ever.

THE PROOF.

"I will love thee, O LORD, my strength." — PSALM xviii 1.

THE CONVICTION

"Ten thousand idols have been tried,
But withering gourds were all;
In God alone our rest is found,
And joys which never pall."

Christ the Life.

"I LIVE, YET NOT I, BUT CHRIST LIVETH IN ME."—*Gal.* ii. 20.

THIS is the secret of spiritual existence; it is immortality begun. The apostle Paul thoroughly understood, that without Christ, he could do nothing; and hence these deep, though simple words. As the body without the soul is dead, and fit only to be buried out of sight, the soul without the Saviour is dead; it has no spiritual vitality, and no relish for the things of God; it is, in truth, dead to him, and all that is heavenly and holy. But when Christ is formed in us the hope of glory, when we become one Spirit with the Lord, it is then that we can do all things through Christ who strengthens us.

Are we near the entrance of the valley of the shadow of death? Christ is our life — of what need we be afraid? Are we surrounded with temptations, so that the germ of spiritual existence is in danger of being crushed? Still Christ lives in the believer; and because that is the case, he need fear no evil: What can prevail against Him in whom all the fulness of the Godhead bodily dwells?

Such is the portion of a ransomed soul — to live in Christ, as well as for him; and let the believer who knows that life say, Is it not one that is hid in God? It is hid from all that would injure it;

nay, it is, in a great measure, hid from the believer himself; for "eye hath not seen, nor ear heard, neither have entered into the heart of man, the things which God has prepared for them that love him." All life besides is a vapor which continueth not, a shadow which declineth, a breath which often expires almost as soon as it is drawn. But Christ is *the life* which responds to man's deepest longings for immortality; and when we are made one Spirit with the Lord, our eternal life has indeed begun. Cling, then, O my soul, to Him who is the life; covet earnestly this highest style of living; and it will be seen that thy existence on earth is just the bud, of which eternity is the ripe fruit. Thou art a minor now; thy majority will begin in our Father's house on high.

THE PROOF.

"I am the way, and the truth, and the life."—JOHN xiv. 6.

THE CONVICTION.

"The Way! Then safely home to God
  Each ransomed soul will rise:
The Truth! Then, trained for heaven by Thee,
  Vain the deceiver's lies.

"The Life! Then death is vanquished now;
  Light gleams within the grave;
While far beyond its gloomy verge,
  Undying glories wave."

The Curse.

"CHRIST HATH REDEEMED US FROM THE CURSE OF THE LAW, BEING MADE A CURSE FOR US." — *Gal.* iii. 13.

OF all the deep things of God, this ranks among the deepest. Gaze into the depth, and attempt to descry its significance.

The Son of God, in whom he is ever well-pleased, was made a curse.

He who did no sin, who was holy, harmless, and undefiled, was made a curse.

He who is the express image of the Father's person, was made a curse.

He who loved the souls of men, and never saw a sorrow which he did not seek to relieve, was made a curse.

He who would not break the bruised reed, nor quench the smoking flax, was made a curse.

He who was the Lord our Righteousness, was made a curse.

The Righteous Branch; the Plant of Renown; the Shepherd; the Hope; the Saviour of Israel — was made a curse.

O, what sin must be, when these are part of its fruits! how hateful to God! how eternally ruinous to man!

And what redemption must be, when it could be accomplished only by the Son of God being made a curse for us! But redemption *has* been accomplished. The Redeemer of Israel bore the load which only omnipotence could sustain; and now our hosannas may be deep — they will be eternal — to Him who came in the name of the Lord to save us.

And what was the nature of that woe which Jesus bore when he died the Just for the unjust? Who shall tell its poignancy, or fathom its depths? All that the sinner should have endured, except the agony of remorse, was the portion of the Saviour; that bitter cup he consented to drink when he undertook to bear his people's sins in his own body on the tree, and addressed himself to the terrible enterprise with the words, "Not as I will, but as thou wilt." Now, my sins, if I rank among the saved, were operating there; and can my attitude ever be too lowly for that, or my self-condemnation too deep?

THE PROOF.

"He that is hanged on a tree, is accursed of God."—DEUT. xxi. 23.

THE HYMN.

"O, raise on earth the song of heaven,
That worthy is the Lamb of God;
Gethsemane and Calvary tell
What woes He bore, what path he trod."

The Triumph.

"YEA, THOUGH I WALK THROUGH THE VALLEY OF THE SHADOW OF DEATH, I WILL FEAR NO EVIL: FOR THOU ART WITH ME; THY ROD AND THY STAFF THEY COMFORT ME."—*Psalm* xxiii. 4.

THE last enemy is death, but the truth as it is in Jesus provides for his perfect overthrow. Many are all their lifetime subject to bondage through fear of death, but the Saviour's triumphs have made ample provision for setting us free from that bondage as well as from every other. And how? What, for example, is it that makes David so bold in the prospect of entering the valley of the shadow of death? How has he succeeded in subduing the terror which haunts so many, and in looking the last enemy so fearlessly in the face? It is a simple truth that has given him the victory. "Thou art with me" explains it all. The Lord his Shepherd was there. As his Shepherd, he tended David with his staff; as his King, he defended him with his sceptre. the rod of his power; and thus encompassed, David could say, "I am comforted."

Now, the same blessing is in store for as many as believe. Is Jesus the life, and do I cling to him in that character? Then death is vanquished. Because he liveth, we shall live also; and neither the grave with its gloom, nor the last enemy with his terrors, need greatly overwhelm my soul. "I will ransom them from the power of the grave," was the promise, and it has been fulfilled. "I will redeem them from death," was the assurance, and He who is the truth has verified it all. "O death, I will be thy plagues," is a clause of the Word which tells how completely the last enemy is destined to be crushed. To consummate the truth, it is written: "O grave, I will be thy destruction." And is not the whole fulfilled? Does not our God keep truth for ever? Is there not imparted to the believer in Jesus a life which knows no death? Nay, is not death abolished by Him who is the resurrection and the life, so that "death is swallowed up in victory?" A grave without a resurrection, and a world without a God, is the dream of many. But because there *is* a God, there is glory, honor, and immortality; and that is the joy of all whom that God has taught.

THE PROOF.

"O death, where is thy sting? O grave, where is thy victory? The sting of death is sin; and the strength of sin is the law. But thanks be to God, which giveth us the victory, through our Lord Jesus Christ."— 1 Cor. xv. 55–57.

THE HYMN.

"Within the portals of the grave
 The Saviour vanquished death;
And now the king of terror quails
 Before the might of faith."

Glory.

"A WITNESS OF THE SUFFERINGS OF CHRIST, AND ALSO A PARTAKER OF THE GLORY THAT SHALL BE REVEALED." — 1 *Pet.* v. 1.

THE glory which awaits the ransomed is the purchase of the Redeemer's agony; and we may thence infer its blessedness. It is the glory of freedom from all sin, both in itself and its effects. It is the glory of being like Christ, and for ever with him. It is not merely freedom from pain, and sorrow, and misery — mere selfishness can prompt such desires; — it is freedom from what occasions these; a glory which eye hath not seen nor heart conceived, but which is all summed up in following the Lamb whithersoever he goes. On such a subject man can only lisp, or lay the hand upon the mouth. Its very grandeur prevents it from being grasped; but this much is certain, perfect felicity, in perfect conformity to the Holy One, awaits the ransomed soul.

Here, then, is the consummation of all things. "It is finished" may now be sounded forth in a sense which is even more profound than when it was uttered on the cross. Paradise is restored — God and man are re-united. Every obstacle to their communion is for ever removed. The soul has got back to its great Original. It is blessed in the retrospect of all that it has endured or enjoyed on earth. It is more blessed still in the full enjoying of God for ever. Every film is removed, every fear is hushed, every sin is pardoned, every stain is washed away; and everlasting life, everlasting glory, becomes the crown and consummation of redemption. True, thousands see no attraction in all these things: and one of the most wonderful things connected with redemption is, that many behold no wonders in the wonderful, no glory in the glorious, no heaven in the heavenly. But be it far otherwise with thee, my soul. Attracted by thy great and mighty Lord, the Wonderful, the Counsellor, walk in light to the home of the holy: there the crown of glory awaits thee, when thou comest to Zion with everlasting joy upon thy head.

THE PROOF.

"And they sung a new song, saying, Thou art worthy to take the book, and to open the seals thereof: for thou wast slain and hast redeemed us to God by thy blood out of every kindred, and tongue, and people, and nation." — REV. v. 9.

THE HYMN.

"O hark! that anthem pealing
  From sainted ones on high,
Their ecstasy revealing —
  'Worthy the Lamb,' they cry.

"O let the earth re-echo,
  In deepest joy, their song —
'Worthy the Lamb,' whose glory
  Thrills all the ransomed throng."

The Heart Kept.

"BUT YE, BELOVED, BUILDING UP YOURSELVES ON YOUR MOST HOLY FAITH, PRAYING IN THE HOLY GHOST, KEEP YOURSELVES IN THE LOVE OF GOD."—*Jude* 20, 21.

IS it not humbling that an effort is needed by man before he can love his God at all! He must watch and pray, and keep his heart with all diligence, before that love can reign in any measure as it should do there. It might be thought that we need only open the eye to look upon the light, to love Him who bade it shine; or on the prolific earth, to love Him who imparted all its riches; or to the heavens above, which so sublimely tell His glory. But ah, no! Man likes not to retain the knowledge of God; and "Ye have been weary of me, O Israel," might still be his complaint. We love every thing around us, but make an exception of Him who is the Author of every good and every perfect gift. The first and great commandment, to love the Lord our God with all the heart, and all the soul, and all the strength and mind, is often, in effect, blotted from the Bible — we do not love him, and we do not regard the operation of his hands.

How, then, is man to be lifted out of this condition? How can he be elevated so as to delight himself in God once more? It is the love of God in Christ which must accomplish that result, and we are to meditate on that till our hearts be affected by the divine display. Just as we keep the departed in our minds, and perpetuate or deepen our love to them by dwelling on the memorials of their love, on their image, or their handiwork, we are to quicken our minds by meditation on the love of God in Christ. He gave his Son to die for us. The sword of his justice awoke against his fellow, that his mercy might flow forth to us. He hid his face from him that it might shine upon us for ever; and when the Spirit of God enables us to see something of the depth of that love, then we love in return. We can resist no longer; and though watchfulness be still needed, before we can "keep ourselves in the love of God" as we should do, yet that love becomes our joy, it is the sunlight of the soul, and the feeling of it is to man's spirit like the breath of spring to the earth.

THE PROOF.

"Delight thyself also in the LORD; and he shall give thee the desires of thine heart." — PSALM xxxvii. 4.

THE CONFESSION.

"We read our heavenly Father's care,
  Within, without, around, above;
Yet, dazzled by his countless gifts,
  Our heart forgets to own his love.

"Each trifle claims that heart by turns,
  And each in turn supplants our God:
Ah, need we wonder though he come
  To chasten with a Father's rod?"

Man's Idolatry—The Antidote.

"AND WHEN THE PEOPLE SAW THAT MOSES DELAYED TO COME DOWN OUT OF THE MOUNT, THE PEOPLE GATHERED THEMSELVES TOGETHER UNTO AARON, AND SAID UNTO HIM, UP, MAKE US GODS, WHICH SHALL GO BEFORE US; FOR AS FOR THIS MOSES, THE MAN THAT BROUGHT US UP OUT OF THE LAND OF EGYPT, WE WOT NOT WHAT IS BECOME OF HIM."—*Exod.* xxxii. 1.

THERE is not a single verse in the Word of God more fraught with instruction than this. The period could be easily counted by hours from the time here referred to, when the people had seen the lightnings, and heard the thunders of Sinai. All that was majestic in God's handiwork, combined with the majesty of his visible presence, to awe and prostrate the Hebrews; and we know that they were terror-stricken—"even Moses did exceedingly fear and quake." To this we must add the deliverance of the Red Sea, with all that preceded and followed that event; and then we have a people placed in circumstances such as were never paralleled in the world.

Yet, amid all that, see how these people forget the God in whose awful presence they stand! See how the visible reigns over the invisible, the gross and the material over the spiritual, the creature above God over all! And see how man's wayward heart wearies of Him on whom every beat which it gives depends! To substitute the image of a four-footed beast for the living God in such circumstances, sheds a lurid light upon the dark soul of man, and tells in a voice as plain as the thunders of Sinai were loud, that our fallen race like not to retain the knowledge of God in the heart.

But other lessons crowd upon us as we gaze in thought upon the calf of Horeb. To hear even Aaron saying, "These be thy gods, O Israel," proclaims aloud how unavailing stupendous miracles are to impress the heart of man, unless the greatest miracle of all — the miracle of the new creation — be wrought upon himself. It is not Sinai with its thunder; it is not the law, with its terrors and demands; it is not agony, however intense, nor sorrows, however crowding; it is not a sea opened for our safe passage; it is not a pillar of cloud or of fire still hovering over us, to guide us in the right way — that will suffice. It is the Spirit of the living God, transforming and illuminating all within, and that alone, that can either make us godly, or keep us so.

THE PROOF.

"And even as they did not like to retain God in their knowledge, God gave them over to a reprobate mind, to do those things which are not convenient." — ROM. i. 28.

THE HYMN.

" Ah, vain the power of man to drive
 The creature from its Maker's throne —
We grasp ten thousand gifts of His,
 And still his love forget to own.

" Poor blinded man will bow the knee
 To vilest things, and call them God,
Till idols piled on idols fill
 That heart, the Spirit's loved abode."

The Destroyer.

"BE SOBER, BE VIGILANT; BECAUSE YOUR ADVERSARY THE DEVIL, AS A ROARING LION, WALKETH ABOUT, SEEKING WHOM HE MAY DEVOUR."—1 *Pet.* v. 8.

AMONG the wonders of redeeming love, it were wrong not to mention the revelation of God's mind regarding the tempter—the accuser of the brethren—that old serpent—the origin of evil on the earth, and of woe unutterable to myriads of the sons of men. Regarding Satanic power, there is much to bewilder and perplex, much that man cannot explain, and need not attempt to fathom. How did the deceiver appear among the sons of God, and obtain a commission to try the patriarch Job? By what power all but omnipotent, or what skill all but omniscient, does he counteract the progress of truth, keeping millions upon millions in bondage, and win an ample title to be deemed the god of this world, the prince of the power of the air? There is much in all that to baffle our inquiries, but the fact we know, at once upon divine authority and from universal experience; and contented with that we must drop into the dust, be silent, and adore.

But "bless the Lord, O my soul!" Though there be much to perplex in the fact that we have a subtle and a crafty spirit against us, there is more to encourage in the fact that we have an omniscient Spirit on our side. If we be tempted in ways which we cannot explain, we are also befriended by One who knows all the avenues to the human heart, all the dangers to which we are exposed, and all the skill which is needed to avert them. He can at once suggest an alarm and tell us the way of safety. He can both excite our fear, and point us to Him who is our shield, our buckler, and high tower. The tempter may turn every object of affection into a snare, every pursuit into a new peril; friendship, business, leisure, activity, the quietude of home, the bustle of the marketplace, the book we read, the words we speak — the very looks which we give or receive — all, all may become a snare and a trap by the craftiness of the deceiver. But are we "sober and vigilant?" Do we press the nearer to our Guardian when we learn our danger? Then He who came to "destroy the works of the devil," will protect us in safety, and teach us to sing, "I will not fear though ten thousand be set round about against me."

THE PROOF.

"Ye are of God, little children, and have overcome them: because greater is he that is in you, than he that is in the world." 1 JOHN iv. 4.

THE HYMN.

"Assaulted by man's deadly foe,
We grasp the Almighty arm;
And with Omniscience to guide,
Even Satan cannot harm."

Deliverance from the Fear of Death.

CHRIST DIED TO "DELIVER THEM WHO THROUGH FEAR OF DEATH WERE ALL THEIR LIFETIME SUBJECT TO BONDAGE."—*Heb.* ii. 15.

ON the field of battle, with passions excited, and a thousand influences at work to goad and stimulate man, multitudes rush upon death without one thought of what is to follow. The horse and his rider there are often alike the creatures of blind impulse. Infuriated rage, or fell hatred, or self-defence, or the groans of the dying, and the ghastliness of the dead, all help to madden men, or hide from their view the terrific results of death beyond the grave.

But how different they who perish inch by inch, it may be during many years of languishing and decay! They have time to estimate aright the king of terrors — to consider all his power, and meditate on the results of his remorseless victory. And for a time that often overwhelms — the soul cannot contemplate the coming struggle without a shudder, or without many tears. "O, the pain, the bliss of dying!" might be poetry on the lips of a heathen emperor when communing with his soul; but when we know that it is "*appointed* unto man once to die, and after death to be judged;" when it is vividly impressed on the mind, that "as the tree falls so must it lie," then trembling often takes hold of the stoutest heart; the question is raised which no power of man can answer: How shall my naked, shivering, sinful soul, appear in the presence of its God?

But, behold just here another instance of the wonders of redeeming love. One has come from heaven to be our life. He says he has "abolished death." He is proclaimed as "the resurrection and the life." We are assured, that he who believeth in Jesus, though he were dead, shall live again; and thus, by line upon line, we are directed to the better life which never ends. A vapor, a shadow, a dream, a phantom, a tale which has been told, is our existence upon earth; glory, honor, and immortality, is our existence beyond the grave; and when faith realizes all that, the soul, formerly bowed down and "in bondage through fear of death," can exclaim, "Though I walk through the valley of the shadow of death, I will fear no evil: for thou art with me; thy rod and thy staff they comfort me."

THE PROOF.

"Jesus said unto her, I am the resurrection and the life; he that believeth in me, though he were dead, yet shall he live." —John xi. 25.

THE HYMN.

"A fleeting phantom is our being here;
  In vain for some abiding joy we pant;
But all is mockery, till the Lord of Life,
  By death abolished, meet our deepest want."

The Heavenly Guide.

"THOU IN THY MERCY HAST LED FORTH THE PEOPLE WHICH THOU HAST REDEEMED: THOU HAST GUIDED THEM IN THY STRENGTH UNTO THY HOLY HABITATION."—*Exod.* xv. 13.

THERE is nothing in the truth of God more offensive to the spirit of the world, than the fact that God is every thing in true religion. He begins it in the soul, he carries it on, and he completes it. Man does not first seek God; it is God that first seeks man. He puts forth his hand to help us, or man would continue self-destroyed and helpless for ever.

The experience of God's people is ever in beautiful accordance with this: "*He* maketh me to lie down;" "*He* leadeth me beside the still waters;" "*He* restoreth my soul again;" "*He* maketh me to walk in the paths of righteousness, and all that for his own name's sake." Such is a portion of the experience of David, and of all whom the Spirit of God is teaching. The Alpha and the Omega of all saving religion is God over all.

And let the soul meditate, for its joy, on the truth of God, with this conviction to guide its meditations.

"'Thou in thy mercy hast led forth thy people." *Thou* hast done it. The movement did not begin with man, but with the Father of Lights. "*In thy mercy,*" moreover; not in consequence of any claim which man had, but solely because that mercy which is deep as floods sought a channel, and found it in the objects of thy choice. The whole began in the fathomless depths of mercy.

And who were thus led? "The people whom *thou* hast redeemed." Slaves before, they are emancipated now, and that because a price more costly than silver or gold has been paid for them by thee.

"Thou hast guided them," farther, "in *thy* strength." Had it not been for that, they would have wandered from the way; but with thy strength made perfect in their weakness, they reach at last "thy holy habitation." Now, it is the question of questions for me to adjust, Am I thus in the way? Is it upon almighty strength that I am leaning? Am I among the redeemed, or still one of the enslaved?

THE PROOF.

"Give ear, O Shepherd of Israel, thou that leadest Joseph like a flock; thou that dwellest between the cherubims, shine forth." — Psalm lxxx. 1.

THE HYMN.

"How wild the sea to fury lashed
  By winter's howling storms!
As wild the soul, as tempest-tost,
  While passion's power deforms.

"How calm the sea when summer smiles
  To hush each wave to rest!
As calm the soul which mercy guides
  To dwell among the blest"

Mercies Deep as Floods.

"AS AN EAGLE STIRRETH UP HER NEST, FLUTTERETH OVER HER YOUNG, SPREADETH ABROAD HER WINGS, TAKETH THEM, BEARETH THEM ON HER WINGS; SO THE LORD ALONE DID LEAD HIM, AND THERE WAS NO STRANGE GOD WITH HIM."— *Deut.* xxxii. 11, 12.

IT is thus that we are taught the loving-kindness of the Lord to his ancient people, and in a picture the most vivid and the most touching, we see his watchfulness and care. He hovers above them like a brooding bird. He never leaves them nor forsakes them. He is their sun and shield; in a pillar of cloud by day, and of fire by night, He guides them by a right way.

But God's ways are equal; he is the same yesterday, to-day, and for ever; and he is doing now what he did in the days of old. By mercy upon mercy, and if need be, correction on correction, he is still leading his pilgrim people through this world to a better. Are they described as children? Then he takes them by the hand and teaches them to go— he nourishes them and brings them up. Are they in distress? Then he chooses them in the furnace Are they assailed by temptations? Then he who touches them, touches the apple of His eye. Are their enemies numerous and strong?. He is greater than all that can be against us. Are they wayward and perverse? He teaches them to behave like a weaned child; they become a willing people in the day of his power.

But why enumerate thus? Does not every soul to which the Bible is something more than a dead letter, discover in it from day to day more of the loving-kindness of the Lord? He knows that the believer, while here below, is like some tender plant brought from the sunny south to our northern clime — unless it be carefully sheltered, it speedily droops, and pines, and dies; or like a taper carried in the breeze, and every moment in danger of being extinguished, the soul in which the grace of God is dwelling, is a frail and tender thing. He therefore keeps his hand ever about it for good. He shelters it from what would nip or extinguish, and tends it with more than a parent's care.

THE PROOF.

"What could have been done more to my vineyard, that I have not done in it? Wherefore, when I looked that it should bring forth grapes, brought it forth wild grapes?" — ISAIAH v. 4.

THE HYMN.

"See that fond bird! she plies each tender wile
  To lure her brood to try their feeble wing.
Now far, now near, she tempts them to the sky,
  Like her to welcome each returning spring.

"So the Great God would train the soul to soar,
  And dwell secure above earth's deadening spell;
His word, his love, his Spirit, and his Son,
  All point to heaven, all, all its glory tell."

The Altogether Lovely.

"THE CHIEFEST AMONG TEN THOUSAND."—*Song* v. 10.

SUCH is the Church's estimate of her Redeemer. To others he has no beauty, that they should desire him. Day passes after day, and mercy after mercy is enjoyed, yet not a thought is dedicated to Him in whom God is ever well pleased, and of whom we read, "Let all the angels of God worship him." But when the Spirit has received the things of Christ, and showed them to us, all that is over: God in Christ becomes the ocean into which the streams of our affections flow — the centre to which they gravitate — the home where they find repose.

And how does God banish our indifference, and bring us under the influence of a heavenly attraction? Not by a mere command, or a mere exercise of power, but by presenting to us a new object of affection, by unveiling its beauty before us, and so winning the heart to love by love. The love of God to sinners, as it is displayed in Christ, attracts us to love God in return. The thought that we have sinned against such tender affection, or grieved one so full of pity, and so ready to forgive, lays us in the dust: and, like the prophet, our confession sometimes is, "I am ashamed, yea, even confounded, because I bear the reproach of my youth."

And it is at this point that He who is altogether

lovely appears in greatest beauty. Our reproach is laid upon him, and in love he bears it away. In doing so, the eye of faith recognizes the forth-putting of his omnipotence as well as the depths of his compassion; as the Sun of Righteousness, he shines in all his glory here; and the simple fact that he died, the just for the unjust, makes him "altogether lovely" indeed, to those whom the Spirit has enlightened to behold his beauty.

And now, my soul, is that beauty beheld by thee? Art thou still among the blind, for whom the Saviour has no comeliness, that we should desire him? Or is it plain that the Brightness of the Father's glory is glorious indeed? Then rejoice with a portion of the joy which is unspeakable and full of glory. We can rarely do more than touch the hem of his garment while here, but we shall be wrapped in the seamless robe hereafter. Nay, more, we shall be like him, and see him as he is.

THE PROOF.

"Lord, to whom shall we go? thou hast the words of eternal life."—JOHN vi. 68.

THE HYMN.

"The sun by day is glorious,
  The stars at eventide,
As silently along yon dome
  In march sublime they glide.

"Yet all that glory fades away,
  It pales before that Sun
Which shines in beauty on the soul—
  God's well-beloved ONE."

The Grand Consummation.

"EYE HATH NOT SEEN, NOR EAR HEARD, NEITHER HAVE ENTERED INTO THE HEART OF MAN, THE THINGS WHICH GOD HATH PREPARED FOR THEM THAT LOVE HIM."—1 *Cor.* ii. 9.

UNLESS we could measure the infinite, or exhaust the inexhaustible, we could not describe all the wonders of redeeming love. It is true that it is with them as it was with the Redeemer himself — many see no beauty in them, that they should be admired. But when the Spirit has revealed them to us, they shine in heaven's own lustre, they are signalized by heaven's own wisdom, and are full to overflowing of its love. Is it love to take sin so utterly away, that it shall be sought for, and nowhere be found? That is made sure in redemption by two immutable things — the word and the oath of God. Is it love to stamp the image of God upon man's soul again? That also is made sure by redemption. Is it love to restore man's happiness, by re-conducting him to his God? That is the grand object of redemption — its terminating point. Is it love to give man the enduring, the eternal, for his portion, when he is prone to grovel among transient things, even while he feels how shadowy they are? All that is in the covenant of redemption, and sure as the word of the Eternal. Is it love to pledge the strength of God to carry poor, frail man onward and upward to glory? That also is provided in the gospel. Is it love to turn that which is by nature like a cage of unclean birds, into a temple of the Holy Ghost? All that is also made sure.

—But we need not attempt to enumerate the whole. Eye hath not seen them, ear hath not heard them; we must wait till that which is perfect be come, before we know them all.

Meanwhile, be encouraged, even amid tears and tribulations, by the gracious invitations of our Redeemer and our God, to profit by this rich provision of love. "The Spirit and the bride say, Come. And let him that heareth say, Come. And let him that is athirst come. And whosoever will, let him take the water of life freely." Be it the prayer, then, of every earnest one—" Come, Lord Jesus, and in thy train bring the exhaustless dowry of blessings made sure by thy love to the redeemed soul.

THE PROOF.

"Beloved, now are we the sons of God; and it doth not yet appear what we shall be: but we know that, when he shall appear, we shall be like him; for we shall see him as he is.— 1 JOHN iii. 2.

THE HYMN.

"Eye hath not seen, and ear hath not heard,
　The bliss which the Saviour in mercy bestowed;
　The raptures of heaven must thrill through the soul,
　Ere we fathom the depths whence redemption has flowed."

THE SHEPHERD OF ISRAEL;

OR,

FAITHFUL IS HE THAT CALLETH YOU

THE SHEPHERD OF ISRAEL.

The Shepherd of Israel.

"THE LORD IS MY SHEPHERD."— *Psalm* xxiii 1.

I AM journeying through a dreary wilderness; but I have a guardian there. One, "like a roaring lion, goeth about seeking whom he may devour;" but another, "the Lion of the tribe of Judah," is mightier far, and the song of the believing soul may therefore be — Greater is he that is for us than all that can be against us.

But the soul requires food as well as defence, and "Give us this day our daily bread," is as needful a prayer as, "Deliver us from evil." Blessed, then, are they who can with one breath exclaim, "The Lord is my shepherd," and add in the next, "I shall not want." And let that heart rejoice which seeks this Lord; for mark how copious is the supply which he provides. "Green pastures" are the emblems of plenty, and "quiet waters" are a synonyme for peace. Plenty and peace, then, or abundance and quietude in which to enjoy it, are made sure to those who have the Lord for their shepherd. He who leads Joseph like a flock, and who leads them gently, is ever a present help; and because He defends, thousands would be too weak to injure.

But how may I know that I am indeed one of the sheep of his pasture? How may I venture to say, the Lord is MY shepherd? He is the good Shepherd, and gives his life for the sheep, but how may I be assured that he is a shepherd to *me?* He himself shall tell. "A stranger my sheep will not follow, but will flee from him, for they know not the voice of a stranger." Is it the case, then, that I know the Shepherd's voice? Is it the Lord that I follow, and do I turn from others, as only the emissaries of him who would destroy? Then he who keepeth Israel has touched my heart; and will lead me by the footsteps of the flock on earth, to the holy mountain, where there is nothing to hurt or to offend, in heaven.

THE PROOF.

"I am the good shepherd: the good shepherd giveth his life for the sheep." — JOHN x. 11.

THE HYMN.

'It is *his* voice? Then, O my soul,
  In silence catch each tone:
Thy woes he feels, thy grief he bears,
  As if they were his own."

The Flock of God.

"FEAR NOT; FOR I HAVE REDEEMED THEE, I HAVE CALLED THEE BY THY NAME; THOU ART MINE." — *Isaiah* xliii. 1.

EVERY thing in the Shepherd of Israel is precious to the soul which follows him, and is designed to make us follow him more and more. He comes to his timid, trembling ones, and his first accents are, "Fear not"—they are designed to encourage and allure. But what is the foundation on which our confidence may rest? "I have redeemed thee," is the gracious reply. Thou art mine, not merely because I created thee, nor merely because every breath thou drawest is a gift from me; but over and beyond all these, I have redeemed thee — and that not with silver and gold, but with the precious blood of Christ, as of a lamb without blemish and without spot. And more still: "I have called thee by thy name; thou art mine." All that is endearing, and all that is close in relationship, thus combine to link the Redeemer and the redeemed together. They are one, through the faithful Word and the life-giving Spirit.

Is this, then, the destiny of my soul? Is it thus that the Holy One deals with those who have rebelled against him? Surely this is heaping coals of fire upon our heads! This is to act not after the manner of man, but of God! It is to show us in foretaste what it will be to be for ever with the Lord. Glory, then, to God in the highest! and be it my life-long endeavor to fulfil the chief end of man — to glorify the Shepherd of Israel, that where he makes his flock to rest, I may rest for ever.

And how insignificant are all earthly things compared with this pursuit of the Chief Good! What though I could count all the stars, or tell all their names? What though I could sum up the drops of the ocean, or measure its waters in the hollow of my hand? What advantage were it though I could walk, as Jehovah does, upon the wings of the wind — if all the while He were still an unknown God, a God afar off; one whom I did not love, or had no prospect of meeting, except as my incensed Judge? — In Him we rest like a sleeping infant on the bosom of its mother; and that rest brings a foretaste of the fulness of joy.

THE PROOF.

"Fear not, little flock; for it is your Father's good pleasure to give you the kingdom." — LUKE xii. 32.

THE PRAYER.

"O Lord of glory! may thy power
My trembling soul defend;
Be thy great name my refuge-tower;
Be thou, O God, my friend!"

The Faithful Promiser.

"HE IS FAITHFUL THAT PROMISED."—*Heb.* x. 23.

HE has promised that sin shall be sought for, but shall not be found; and He is faithful to "do as he has said."

He has promised, that in six troubles, yea, in seven, He will be present with us; and we may rely on his faithfulness to perform it.

"When thou passest through the waters, I will be with thee; and through the rivers, they shall not overflow thee," is another assurance. Now, "hath he spoken," and will he not perform?

"Thy Maker is thy husband," is the declaration of the Holy One; and as He cannot alter what has gone out of his mouth, we may both plead the promise and expect its fulfilment. Though it was made to the church of old, every believer may plead it still, and in pleading it rejoice. We are weak and need defence—He is at our right hand. We are helpless and need a shield—He delivers. We have countless foes—He is mightier than they all. For all that, we have his own guaranty, an assurance as stable as the everlasting hills; and when we restore to the Holy One that confidence which Adam withdrew when he believed the father of lies, all will be well again.

"I will pour out my Spirit upon you," is another

gracious intimation from Him who is the Truth; and with that to animate and gladden, we may go forward, rejoicing in the strength which the truth supplies. Surely it is enough to know that "God is faithful, by whom ye were called unto the fellowship of his Son Jesus Christ our Lord;" or if that be not enough. is not the soul still distempered? Is not God still dishonored, and what marvel then though man be still unhappy?

"There is no condemnation for them that are in Christ;" "Sin shall not have dominion over you;" "My grace shall be sufficient for you, my strength shall be perfected in your weakness:" these, and a crowd of exceeding great and precious promises, are scattered through the Word of God, as numerous and bright as the stars in the midnight sky; and as they are all founded on the truth, they are all to be rested on as the Rock of Ages. Repose there, then, O my soul. All is immutable as the word of the Eternal; and having His promises as the basis of your hope, you may glory in them, like those that divide the spoil.

THE PROOF.

"All the promises of God in him are yea, and in him **Amen, unto** the glory of God by us."—2 Cor. i. 20.

THE HYMN.

"On the truth I repose, nay, on thee, O my God,
    For thou art the Truth to my soul;
No shadow, no phantom, no fiction of earth,
    Shall rival thy gracious control."

Everlasting Remembrance.

"BEHOLD I HAVE GRAVEN THEE UPON THE PALMS OF MY HANDS."—*Isaiah* xlix. 16.

WE have many hard thoughts of God. A guilty and therefore timid conscience, prompts fear upon fear, and doubt upon doubt. But to silence them all, He who is the guardian of Israel has given assurance upon assurance, and none more encouraging than this, "I have graven thee on the palms of my hands." Does a mother love her child? Is she sleepless in her vigilance, and inventive in her care for his welfare? So will I be towards thee. But a mother may forget her child; there are mothers who, like the ostrich, can utterly neglect their offspring. But I will not forget thee. To assure thee of that, "I have graven thee on the palms of my hands;" and as the hands are ever before the eyes, thou art ever before me. The immutability of God is thus thy pledge—immutability in league with love.

Now, with an assurance so full of consolation, what can become a believer so well, as the exclamation, "Sing, O heavens; and be joyful, O earth; and break forth into singing, O mountains; for the Lord hath comforted his people, and will have mercy upon his afflicted?" Far from forgetting us amid our waywardness, or leaving us to be filled with the fruits of our own devices, our covenant God has given us promise upon promise, to assure, console, and uphold us. I am poor and needy, but the Lord thinketh on me; I am unstable as water, but in the Lord have I both righteousness and strength; I am less than the least of all saints, if I be a saint at all; but where is the portion of the Word in which it is written, thy salvation depends on thy being a great saint, or even on thy having great faith? It is to *faith*, and not to *great faith*, that the promises are made; and though our faith might be great, and should be great, yet faith like a grain of mustard-seed can take hold of Christ, and in his strength we can do all things. That is the spirit in which the Holy One would animate and cheer us. Be his simple Word, then, the basis of our hope; and our faith, like the morning light, will grow brighter and brighter, till it be lost in vision for ever.

THE PROOF.

"When my father and my mother forsake me, then the Lord will take me up." — PSALM xxvii. 10.

THE RESOLUTION.

"I grasp the promise of my God
  His power shall be my stay;
O, need that soul be desolate,
  Where grace holds welcome sway?"

# Salvation Made Sure.

"LOOKING UNTO JESUS." — *Heb.* xii. 2.

IS the soul still unpardoned, and bowed down by the condemnation of God? Then behold the Lamb, that there may be "no condemnation."

Is the soul troubled, and anxious, lest it should perish in its sins? Then look to Him, that the burden which weighs you down may be utterly removed.

Does the soul remember the time when it was better with it than now — when this world had less power to enthrall, and the next more power to elevate and attract? Then behold the Lamb, and seek grace to return and do your first works, that the soul may again rejoice.

Is the soul at ease in Zion, and exposed to the woe denounced upon those who are so? Then look to Jesus, that he may rescue from the fearful pit and the miry clay, into which you are in danger of sinking again.

Or has the soul some reason to hope that it is growing in grace? Is Christ more precious, is sin more hateful, is holiness more sought, is heaven more in your thoughts, is the spell of earth weaker than it was a year ago? Then look to Him who takes away the sin of the world, for strength to perfect the triumph. His grace began it, and the same grace must complete it; for grace must have all the glory, and that is the secret of the conquest of sin.

Or is the soul weeping beside the dying, or mourning for the dead? Is the heart like to break, because some much-loved object has been torn from your embrace, and carried to the narrow house? Then look to the Saviour, and be soothed amid it all. He was the Man of Sorrows and is still our peace; he sends the Comforter; and though trials were to come as thick upon the soul as they did upon the stricken Job, grace would enable the believer, even amid tears, to say with the patriarch, "Though he slay me, yet will I trust in Him."

Hast thou learned, or art thou learning, my soul, this simple lesson of "beholding the Lamb;" or is the command to do so only so many syllables to thee? O do not forget that thy eternity depends on looking in faith to the Saviour of the lost.

THE PROOF.

" And looking upon Jesus as he walked, he saith, Behold the Lamb of God."—JOHN i. 36.

THE HYMN.

"As pales the star at sunrise,
  So fades each mortal thing,
When the soul, illumed from heaven,
  First sees its Saviour-King.

"Lo, his the hand that guides us,
  His grace our guilt forgives,
Look, then, to him, ye laden,
  The soul, in looking, lives."

The All-Sufficient One.

"COME, SEE A MAN WHICH TOLD ME ALL THINGS THAT EVER I DID: IS NOT THIS THE CHRIST?"—*John* iv. 29.

WHEN a portrait has been painted by the hand of a master, one peculiarity of it is, that it seems to gaze upon every one who sees it. Though ten thousand times ten thousand could contemplate it at once, it would still appear to be calmly returning the look of each.

And so with the Saviour of sinners. It was not merely the woman of Samaria who felt that he knew all her history and condition. It is the same with every soul that comes seriously and solemnly, as for life and death, to deal with the Son of God. He looks us through and through, and with the eye of his omniscience intently fixed upon us, he is prepared to deal with us, according to our various conditions. He knows all our sins, and has mercy to pardon them; our weakness, and has grace to turn it into strength; our temptations, and is prepared to give us the victory over them all; our enemies, and will subdue them; our sorrows, and will either soothe them, or give us patience to acquiesce in his holy awards. In a word, in whatever condition the believer may be, the Saviour has been there before him; there to turn tears into joy at last; to make our very trials minister to our peace; to compass us about with songs of deliverance, and make *all* things work together for our good.

Such is the Saviour provided for sinners. Now, the eye of some immortal being is running along these syllables, which we know, upon God's authority, to be true, and let me ask — Is that Saviour a Saviour to *thee?* Hast thou found out his exquisite adaptation to the soul? As face answers to face in a glass, the gospel is adapted to man, whether we see it or no. O make sure, then, that the Saviour provided is thy Saviour; and then go up through the wilderness rejoicing. In the *written* Word, the soul which is born from above finds a light to the feet, and a lamp to the path; but in the Word *made flesh,* it finds all that it can ever need either in time or for ever.

THE PROOF.

"Jesus knew from the beginning who they were that believed not, and who should betray him." — JOHN vi. 64.

THE HOPE.

"No deed, no word, no secret thought
Escapes that flaming eye;
But not less true this blessedness —
God hears the contrite sigh.

"And as the lake at summer's eve
Reflects the sun and sky,
That soul may feel the Saviour shed
His soothing sympathy."

The Sanctuary of the Soul.

"I WILL BE TO THEM AS A LITTLE SANCTUARY."—*Ezek.* xi. 16.

IT is thus that He against whom sinners have rebelled continues to deal with them — thus that he seeks to reclaim them, and prepare a people to himself. His love he cannot take from the sheep of his pasture, nay, having loved them with an everlasting love, he bears with them amid countless wanderings. By his long-suffering he leads them to repentance; and though he will be avenged on their sins, he will save themselves, though it should be as by fire.

And O, mark with what kindness he undertakes to be as a little sanctuary to them in the time of trouble! He will not connive at their transgressions; for sin, which is ever hateful to the Holy One, is hateful most of all in his own children. But still he will open a city of refuge for them. He will provide a hiding-place from the storm. He will cover them as with the hollow of his hand. His own gracious words are: "I will be a little sanctuary unto them" — I, against whom they have rebelled — I, whom they have grieved by preferring my creatures to myself — I, who had set my heart upon them, while they would none of me — even I will be their sanctuary and hiding-place. In me they shall have rest, though they have wearied me with their transgressions, and made me to serve with their sins.

Surely this is not after the manner of man! Surely this is saving to the uttermost! "When thine enemy hungers, feed him; when he is athirst, give him drink," is the divine command; and does not the Holy One do as he commands? He is himself the sanctuary of his people. He *will* make them dwell there, and adorn them at last with the beauties of his holiness; and even the King eternal, immortal, and invisible, cannot do more for the souls of the sinful. They may still prefer some lying vanity, or place their confidence in a creature rather than in God over all. But when He says "come," do we flee to the Rock? When He opens up a way, do we hasten along it to himself? Then let the heart of him rejoice that seeks the Lord. He who began the good work will carry it on to perfection; and, even though the last enemy were assailing, the soul would find a sanctuary in its God.

THE PROOF

"Sanctify the Lord of hosts himself, and let him be your fear, and let him be your dread. And he shall be for a sanctuary.'—Isa. viii. 13, 14.

THE REFUGE.

"How safe the timid, trembling soul,
  Beneath his sheltering wing!
Though Satan tempt, or death should **frown**,
  That soul may triumphs sing."

The Rock of our Confidence.

"GREATER IS HE THAT IS IN YOU, THAN HE THAT IS IN THE WORLD." — 1 *John* iv. 4.

SHOULD such a man as I flee? was the question asked by one of old, and the same question may still be asked by every believing soul.

Should I flee, when omnipotence is on my side?

Should I flee, when He who called the world into being is my buckler, and my high tower?

Should I flee, when the whole armor of God is laid down for my use, and when I have directions the most explicit for employing it?

Or if Omnipotence be not enough to encourage and tranquillize me, then let the appeal be to Omniscience to reënforce it. My God knows my temptations as well as my weakness. He sees how numerous are my enemies, and that my dangers are in proportion. He understands my thoughts afar off, and is ready to make me more than a conqueror in my saddest hour. Why, then, art thou cast down, my soul? what should discourage thee? The friend of my affections; the child of my soul; the brother of my inmost confidence: the friend with whom I have often taken sweet counsel — is swept away with a stroke, and the trial threatens to crush me. Yet why should it do so, when my God and Saviour is my Rock?

Again; the rude world, with its resistless current, threatens to sweep me away, so that I often exceedingly fear and quake — it seems impossible to prevail where enemies are at once so numerous and so powerful. But let the agitated soul fall back on the divine assurance, " Greater is he that is in us, than he that is in the world;" and when that word is believed, it will impart a portion at once of the peace and the strength of Jehovah. " For who is God save the Lord? or who is a Rock save our God?"—" He is the Rock, and his work is perfect," and under His shadow, we are safe from Satan, the world, and the flesh. Unbelief clings to what acts like the torpedo, benumbing and deadening whatever it strikes; but faith lays hold of One who imparts his own strength to all who repose upon Him, and that is the secret of the believer's triumph. Take that secret to guide the soul, and conquer. Neglect or ignore it, and death ensues.

THE PROOF.

"The Lord liveth; and blessed be my Rock; and let the God of my salvation be exalted."—PSALM xviii. 46.

SAFETY.

" Mark yon proud embattled host
  Rush on in fiery shock;
  They seek to vanquish God's redeemed,
    But find He is their Rock.

" Ten thousand times ten thousand,
  Recoil when he defends;
  And feeble arms grow mighty,
    When Omnipotence befriends."

Joy Restored.

"THOUGH THOU WAST ANGRY WITH ME, THINE ANGER IS TURNED AWAY, AND THOU COMFORTEDST ME."—*Isaiah xii.*

THE Holy One might well be angry — angry in proportion as the blessings which he had bestowed were slighted; but he could not keep his anger for ever; nay, it was turned away. The death which made reconciliation for the sins of the people, was contemplated by Him who cannot look on sin; and peace with God through our Lord Jesus Christ was the result.

And how often is it thus in the history of the soul! When it is first awakened, or first compelled to face the question, "What must I do to be saved?" it frequently feels as if that eye which glares so ominously on sin, were scorching it with an angry glance. But when that agitated one has been taught to "believe in the Lord Jesus Christ," then anger is turned away, and it is comforted, even by Him who was dreaded as an enemy before.

Or when a child of God has fallen into sin, when he has gone back to the world, and returned to folly; then again the light of our Father's countenance is darkened with a frown. But are we humbled under it? Do we flee once more to the fountain opened for sin? Do we walk softly, and ashamed at the remembrance of our folly? Then

God comforts us again — He speaks peace; His anger is turned away, and he delights in mercy.

Or does faith grow weak, and slip from the rock of truth, to the sandbank or the wave of feeling? Then again, God seems to forsake us, or rather we forsake him; and our joy is necessarily turned into mourning. But does faith resume its sway? Does it rest again upon the simple truth, independent of all suspicions and all hard thoughts? Then, when our covenant with him by sacrifice is renewed, we also renew our youth like the eagle. We joy in God, while the consolations of the Comforter are again imparted to the soul. — Such is the course along which many a child of God is led to glory. They would draw back to perdition, were they forsaken by God; but at one time, the terrors of the Lord, and at another time his smile and his love, urge them onward to their appointed home. Few of us can bear perpetual sunshine: we need the biting frost as well as the refreshing dew; and both are in mercy sent.

THE PROOF.

"Blessed is he whose transgression is forgiven, whose sin is covered." — PSALM xxxii. 1.

THE CONVICTION.

"As summer's sun may clouded be,
  Or autumn's riches blighted;
So God may frown; but still his own
  Are to their Lord united."

The Gift Received.

"BEHOLD, GOD IS MY SALVATION; I WILL TRUST, AND NOT BE AFRAID: FOR THE LORD JEHOVAH IS MY STRENGTH AND MY SONG; HE ALSO IS BECOME MY SALVATION."—*Isaiah* xii. 2.

WE should not fail to notice here, how *appropriating* is the language which is employed. It is not merely salvation — it is *my* salvation; and the sentiment is twice repeated, as if the soul would press out all the blessedness which it contains. Nor is even that enough: It is added, "The Lord JEHOVAH is my strength and my song." Not a creature — that would not have sufficed; not one of the "gods many" to which the Gentiles appealed — that would have been only a refuge of lies. It was accordingly the Lord JEHOVAH, the eternal I AM, that was the strength and the song of the prophet, or the souls which he personified.

And why should our faith not be as appropriating still? Is the Lord's word less true? Are his promises fewer? Is he less able, or less willing to save? Nay, He is the Lord, he changes not; and we might therefore repose as peacefully on his mercy, as did the believer to whom this text refers. Or more than this: not merely are we at liberty thus to repose with certainty on God — we are commanded to "give diligence to make our calling and election *sure*." Not a peradventure; not a hope which may end in despair; not a salvation which may prove to be perdition; but something sure, definite, and fixed, is what the believer should aim at; and he is satisfied with something less than God has placed within his reach, who sits down contented with a peradventure, when certainty might be enjoyed. Freely take, then, what God so freely offers. Do not turn the glad tidings of great joy into a cause of sorrow. Let the Lord Jehovah be your song, and the unchanging blessedness will begin even amid the sorrows and the crosses of earth. Look upon the rainbow spanning the earth in its beauty, and whence that lovely form? The dark cloud behind it — the rain drops and the sun are its cause — and in like manner, man may often be most blessed when his trials and his tears are most abundant. If these trials compel him to appeal to the Comforter, if they estrange him from the things which perish in the using, and warn him to flee in hope to the appointed stronghold, they are like ministering angels sent on errands of mercy to the soul.

THE PROOF.

" Therefore the rather, brethren, give diligence to make your calling and election sure; for if you do these things, ye shall never fall." — 2 Pet. i. 10.

THE WELCOME.

" My life, my joy, my strength, and hope,
My Righteousness and peace —
Be that the language of my soul,
Till all my doubtings cease."

Streams in the Desert.

"WITH JOY SHALL YE DRAW WATER OUT OF THE WELLS OF SALVATION." — *Isaiah* xii. 3

THE Shepherd of Israel has promised that bread shall be provided and water made sure: and here is a fulfilment of the assurance. The wells of salvation were to yield that water, as heaven itself was to supply the bread of life — the Saviour.

And the purposes of these waters are twofold. First, they purify. Till that be done, there can be no blessedness for man; even the Shepherd of Israel cannot impart true joy, as long as we continue in sin. They are the pure who are the peaceful; they shall even see God.

But the waters which the wells of salvation yield, serve a second purpose — they refresh while they purify. Streams in the desert, rivers of water in a dry place, and similar figures, are often employed to set forth the blessedness of Gospel times, and this is the meaning of the words before us. Now, how blessed that all this is free! without money and without price it may be enjoyed. Nay, various influences are brought to bear upon us to induce us to enjoy it. "The Spirit says, Come;" that is, He whom the Saviour sent to show us what salvation is, would guide us to the fountain. "And the Bride says, Come;" that is, the Church takes up the appeal, and presses it upon all who will listen. "And he who heareth is to say, Come;" that is, all are to use their influence to bring sinners to the wells of salvation. "He that is athirst is to come," for here alone can thirst be really quenched — everywhere else we attempt to quench it with brine. "And whosoever will, is to come." Without limit, and without restriction, all may come; all are needy, and therefore all are welcome, when the God of grace spreads a table in the wilderness, and opens up streams in the desert.

Now, is not this like the very sunshine of heaven beaming upon the soul? What more can we ever expect to enjoy, till we dwell on the banks of that stream which gladdens the city of our God? There are not two heavens for men although they often vainly dream that there are. There is but one — This is the land of our pilgrimage, and happy are they who are using earth only as their path to glory — supported or encouraged by the way, but never supposing that that way is their home.

THE PROOF.

"There is a river, the streams whereof shall make glad the city of God, the holy place of the tabernacles of the most High."— Psalm xlvi. 4.

THE JOY.

"O, why should the hearts of believers despond,
　As if from their God they were driven?
Nay, welcome the joy which he graciously sheds,
　To cheer the steep pathway to heaven."

The Spirit of Praise.

"AND IN THAT DAY SHALL YE SAY, PRAISE THE LORD, CALL UPON HIS NAME, DECLARE HIS DOINGS AMONG THE PEOPLE, MAKE MENTION THAT HIS NAME IS EXALTED."—*Isaiah* xii 4.

BLESSINGS beyond what can be counted are enjoyed by the children of men. Every breath is adding to their number, both as regards the body and the soul, and yet, as if we had a title to them all and more, we seize upon the gift, and forget to praise the Giver. As when the ten lepers were cleansed, only one returned to thank his deliverer, few are ready now with thanksgiving for the mercies which they enjoy in such ample abundance.

And yet in the Word of God we have line upon line to teach us to praise. How earnest is "the man after God's own heart," that we should be much in that employment, and how largely does he exemplify in his own practice, the lesson which he taught to others! In the same spirit, in the verse before us, " Praise the Lord," is one invitation, " Proclaim his name," is another, " Declare his doings among the people," is a third, and " Make mention that his name may be exalted," is a fourth. The prophet cannot be sufficiently urgent. He sees or he feels so much for which we ought to praise our God, that he presses, and returns to press the privilege upon us. And surely they forsake their own mercies who neglect it

— they multiply their own joys who have learned "in every thing to give thanks" — to pour out the heart in prayer for mercies needed, and in praise for mercies received. Learn, then, my soul, to enjoy this hallowing privilege. It will bring thee near to God, and prepare thee for more and more of his mercies. Think how much thou receivest, and all undeserved, in the course of a single day or hour; and if that do not draw forth thy praise, thy spirit is not Isaiah's; the doubt may arise, "Is God recognized and glorified by me at all?"

It cannot be doubted that the religion of Jesus is designed to make us happy. The very God of peace would thereby diffuse a portion of the joy of heaven through man's heart upon earth. And how can that be better promoted than by cherishing the spirit of praise — by recognizing God's goodness in every gift, and thanking him for it by acknowledging our own unworthiness, and the Lord's loving-kindness! When life on earth is thus a hymn, existence in heaven will be one long hosanna.

THE PROOF.

"Abounding therein with thanksgiving." — Col. ii. 7.

THE ANTHEM.

"Exult, O my soul, in a Saviour's grace,
Let thy heart with his praises run o'er;
Be my life a long anthem of praise to that love
Which has opened the heavenly store."

Scarcely Saved.

"IF THE RIGHTEOUS SCARCELY BE SAVED, WHERE SHALL THE UNGODLY AND THE SINNER APPEAR?"—1 *Pet.* iv. 18.

NO opinion is more common among the unthinking sons of men, than that salvation is easy, and that to "work it out with fear and trembling," is a superfluous injunction in the Word of God. Compliance with a few outward forms; some cold and decent formalities; whitewashing the outside of the cup and the platter;—these and similar things are deemed sufficient by thousands to prepare them for eternity, in as far as they think of their souls at all.

But he who leads Joseph like a flock, is careful to undeceive us here, and impress us with the conviction that, though salvation be easy as regards the power of God, it is difficult as regards the waywardness of man. "The righteous shall scarcely be saved;" "It will be so as by fire;" "Not every one that saith unto me, Lord, Lord, shall enter the kingdom of heaven;" "Work out your own salvation with fear and trembling;" or, "Beware lest a promise of entering in being left to us, any of you should seem to come short of it"—these are some of the texts by which he who knows what is in man, would warn us to make salvation sure. And happy they who are warned, who lean on the strength and take counsel of the wisdom which the Holy One provides! Have I, then, **acted** thus? Is that strength my resting-place? Then it will be perfected in my weakness. Is that wisdom my counsellor? Then coming from above it will guide me thither, and the joy of the Lord will be my strength for ever. Meanwhile, I may comply with the prophet's lesson, and "sing unto the Lord, for he hath done excellent things; this is known in all the earth."

Amid the countless difficulties which hinder our entering on the narrow way, or impede our progress after we have entered, the friendships of the world rank among the most embarrassing. In the view of these we may well ask — Who then can be saved? But while we ask the question, let us not overlook the reply — "With God all things are possible." He can carry us with triumph through an host of adversaries, and the friend who sticketh closer than a brother, is revealed for that very end.

THE PROOF.

"And again I say unto you, It is easier for a camel to go through the eye of a needle, than for a rich man to enter into the kingdom of God." — *Matt.* xix. 24.

THE HOPE.

"The eternal Spirit is my strength,
  Were he to change, I perish;
But changeless still, the hope of life
  He bids me freely cherish."

The Peace of God.

"BE CAREFUL FOR NOTHING: BUT IN EVERY THING BY PRAYER AND SUPPLICATION, WITH THANKSGIVING, LET YOUR REQUEST BE MADE KNOWN UNTO GOD. AND THE PEACE OF GOD, WHICH PASSETH ALL UNDERSTANDING, SHALL KEEP YOUR HEARTS AND MINDS THROUGH CHRIST JESUS." — *Phil.* iv. 6, 7.

THE abundance of the teeming earth is but a type of the affluence with which God has provided consolation or joy for his people. It is true, many of them walk in sackcloth, and sit in darkness, seeing no light. They hang down their heads like a bulrush. They mourn in their complaint, and make a noise. As if the Saviour had come to immure or imprison, instead of opening the prison doors to them that are bound, many walk in chains; they seem even to be afraid to be happy.

Yet O, how beautiful is the provision which God has made for happiness to the believer! Great peace, perfect peace, Christ's peace, and the very peace of God — seem to be the gradations by which the Holy One guides us to blessedness; for His mind obviously is, that man should be led back to Eden, or that he should delight himself in the abundance of peace, as pardoned and accepted by his God.

And the word of God makes all that not merely a privilege, but a duty. We are enjoined to be careful, that is, anxious or fretful, about nothing.

We are to commit our way unto God, with prayer for his grace and thanksgiving for his gifts. We are to cast all our cares upon him who cares for us; and when our burden is thus cast upon the Lord, he will keep us in perfect peace, the very peace of God. Now, let the soul rejoice that all this is made sure through Him in whom all the promises are yea and amen. "Through Jesus Christ our Lord," is the crowning mercy of all. Upon that the soul should repose, and practise there the deep lesson of the apostle, "I can do all things through Christ who strengtheneth me; I have learned in whatsoever state I am to be therewith content." How blessed they whom the Spirit of God is guiding thus! A crust may be their richest fare; a hovel may be their home; or their soul may dwell in a frail tabernacle which is slowly but daily decaying—but as an heir of glory, such a man is rich indeed—and in the world of realities all will be put right.

THE ASSURANCE.

"My God shall supply all your needs according to his riches in glory by Christ Jesus."— PHIL. iv. 19.

THE HYMN.

"O how exhaustless the believer's store!
  The grace, the peace, the very life of God,
All, all are his, that he may fear no more,
  But walk in triumph to his blest abode."

"Know the Lord."

"THEN SHALL WE KNOW, IF WE FOLLOW ON TO KNOW THE LORD."—*Hosea* vi. 3.

NOT merely by beginning to inquire. Not merely by running well for a time. Not merely by turning our faces Zionward for a season. Not by a few spasmodic efforts, as if one struggle or a few could take the kingdom of heaven by force. But by commencing, by continuing, by pressing into the kingdom, by never wearying in well-doing, by never thinking that we have already attained, or are already perfect, by going on unto perfection, and holding the beginning of our confidence steadfast unto the end — it is by that process that we arrive at the knowledge of God, in his mercy, his compassion, his power and willingness to save us in Christ.

But when we do set our face thus steadfastly towards Jerusalem, O how firm and valid are our guaranties, how infallible the assurance that we shall be guided in a right way to a city which hath foundations! Jehovah himself is our strength, his truth is a light to our path, and the consolations which he sheds around us cheer us on the way. Correction comes to stimulate, harassing cares are sent to rouse us. Dangers arise to show us the need of the heavenly Shield; but amid all these he is at our right hand, and we grow in knowledge as we grow in days.

Look back, then, my soul, on the days that are past. As in the sight of the Heart-searcher, does it appear that progress has been made? Art thou following on to inherit life, or drawing back to perdition? Having put thy hand to the plough, art thou looking back, and so forfeiting the harvest of glory; or art thou sowing well, and preparing to reap well, that is, sowing to the Spirit, and expecting the fruit to be unto everlasting life?

On the sea-beach after a storm we sometimes see the fragments of some stately vessel, or portions of her cargo cast upon the shore. All tells of disaster and death, and the heart sinks at the thought of the strong men who there found a watery grave. Now that spectacle finds a parallel in the case of those who make shipwreck of the faith; who run well, but are hindered after a season, and so draw back to perdition.

THE PROOF.

"Acquaint thyself with God, and be at peace; thereby good shall come unto thee."—Job xxii. 21.

THE HYMN.

"Onward! be that the Christian's cry,
Upward! there fix the Christian's eye,
A throne! be that the Christian's aim,
And, Welcome Heaven! his last acclaim."

The Mysterious Life.

"YOUR LIFE IS HID WITH CHRIST IN GOD."— *Col.* iii. 8.

THE believer's life is hid from the worldly man's eye; it is something which he cannot understand, or with which he cannot sympathize. To walk with God, to endure or to enjoy as seeing God who is invisible, to seek habitual communion with Him, to be happy when he is near, but restless and unsatisfied when the light of his countenance is darkened — all these are utterly shadowy or strange to the majority of men. But when our hearts have been touched by a heavenly power, and turned to heavenly things, then all mysterious as the joys of a child of God might *once* appear, they become clear and exhilarating now — the very heart is made glad by them. It does not need to wander from object to object, or scene to scene, asking "Who will show us any good?" or exclaiming, "They have taken away my gods, and what have I left?" Nay, that heart finds repose, and a perfectly suitable portion, in the hidden things of God. They are hidden from the wise and the prudent, but they are revealed unto babes; and even amid the cares and troubles of earth, such a soul feels that it has more than it can ask. It has returned to its Father's home and heart. It is now perfectly blessed in kind, and waits for the time when it shall be perfect also in degree.

While the believer has a life which is thus hid with Christ in God, or joys with which the world cannot intermeddle, he has also a life which is seen and read of all men. They have reason to take knowledge of him that he has been with Jesus, and that he is of a different spirit from them, because his presence is often a check to their folly and their sin. These are the living epistles of the Lord Jesus; they are, in one sense, the Lord's remembrancers; they are the salt of the earth, or cities set upon a hill. They are God's witnesses like the Jews of old; and there lives force upon the notice of an unwilling world, both the holy goodness and the holy severity of God. Their hidden life ministers strength for their public duty, as the germ of immortality is also the germ of personal holiness in the ransomed of the Lord.

THE PROOF.

"I thank thee, O Father, Lord of heaven and earth, because thou hast hid these things from the wise and prudent, and hast revealed them unto babes." — MATT. xi. 25.

THE HYMN.

" The faithful soul's mysterious joy
    Eludes the worldly eye;
But grace shed o'er that soul by God,
    Unveils the mystery."

Sorrowing, yet Rejoicing.

"IN ALL THEIR AFFLICTION HE WAS AFFLICTED." — *Isaiah* lxiii. 9.

IT is by such a scripture that we are enabled to read the very heart of our God. "So he was their Saviour," precedes these words; and we thus learn how thoroughly he sympathizes with those who mourn. His people are an afflicted and a poor people: He chooses them in the furnace of affliction, and the man that has seen affliction is the object of his peculiar care. Though his redeemed are often destitute, afflicted, and tormented — though the afflictions of the righteous are many — though they must often receive the word with much affliction; in short, though they be often "bound in affliction and iron," the Man of Sorrows still sympathizes with them. He suffers in our suffering; He waits to deliver; and as soon as the rod of correction has accomplished the purpose for which it was employed, it will be laid aside or consumed. It is sin that draws down affliction, and does it lead us to hate sin and love holiness? Then it has accomplished its design, and the peaceable fruits of righteousness will be the result.

I cleave, then, to the Man of Sorrows. I would rather suffer affliction with the people of God, than enjoy the pleasures of sin. When I am rebuked,

I would endure chastening without impatience, and look for profit in hope. I would remember that "the Lord hath seen the affliction of his people," and though he give them the bread of affliction to eat, I would still say, "Happy is the man whom the Lord correcteth." I would make every affliction a new errand to his throne. Thither I would go for the Spirit, the Comforter, for the sympathy of the Man of Sorrows; and then I am sure that, sooner or later, as one whom his mother comforts, the Lord will comfort his people. O holy Saviour, "look upon mine affliction:" "I cry to thee out of my affliction:" "I am holden in the cords of affliction." "But this is my comfort there, that thy Word hath quickened me." Free me, then, O God, my Saviour, from my pain; let thy Spirit comfort and sustain; but O, make me yet more anxious to profit by my sorrow, than to have it removed. May it be to me a proof of thy love, not of thy wrath; so shall I praise thee even for my tears.

THE PROOF.

"We glory in tribulation also: knowing that tribulation worketh patience; and patience experience; and experience hope." — Rom. v. 3. 4.

THE TRIUMPH.

"Come grief and tears, come crushing woe:
  If grace come with the load,
Then welcome all — they snap the chains
  Which keep me from my God."

The Path of Peril.

"QUENCH NOT THE SPIRIT."—1 *Thess.* v. 19.

EVERY sin has a tendency to that fearful consummation. Do I read the Word of God, without laying to heart its weighty warnings? I am grieving the Spirit, and that grieving may prove the prelude to quenching him. Do I kneel down in prayer, and yet only mock God because my heart is not engaged in his service? Again I am grieving the Spirit, and that may end in quenching Him who will not always strive with the children of men. Am I adding sin to sin, in spite of warnings, and expostulations, and entreaties? I am on the way to quench the Holy Spirit: I do always resist Him. Do I feel my conscience remonstrating against my ways, while yet I go forward? Have I my fears as to whether my soul be safe, while I hush all these fears, and go blindly on unwarned? Then, I am in the way to perpetrate that sin which consists in quenching the Holy One; and in that case will be left undisturbed, without compunction, or alarm. "He is joined to his idols," becomes the verdict of Jehovah on such a soul.

But do I yield to the holy movements of the Spirit? In prayer do I cry to him to help my infirmities? In reading the Word, is it my petition that He would illumine the sacred page? In the ordinary intercourse of life — among friends, brethren, strangers, everywhere — is it my heart's desire to be guided by the Holy Spirit, and sanctified wholly, even till I have no will but God's? Then I am honoring the Spirit of all grace; living in the Spirit, I am also walking in the Spirit, and He will show me the things of Christ; the Spirit of the Lord will impart liberty indeed. He will make the soul one Spirit with the Lord; in a word, "the kingdom of God is within" that soul, or "righteousness, and peace, and joy in the Holy Ghost." Now, is not he duped and deceived, who consents to forego that blessedness? But is not he taught of God, and made wise indeed, who covets earnestly these best gifts, and lives as the great Fountain of holiness would have him?

THE PROOF.

"Whosoever shall speak a word against the Son of man, it shall be forgiven him: but unto him that blasphemeth against the Holy Ghost, it shall not be forgiven." — LUKE xii. 10.

THE HYMN.

"Each movement of the Holy One,
Each joy, each hope, and fear,
Through his own grace I cherish,
And smile through every tear."

The Great Calm.

"IT IS I." — *Matt.* xiv. 27.

BY these words the Saviour would dispel every fear. If he be near, it is enough; no evil thing can befall us, no plague can come near our dwelling.

Is the believer struggling with indwelling sin, and does it seem as if it would sweep him away with the force of a resistless current? The Saviour approaches: "It is I," is heard, and all fear is hushed.

Or is the believer assailed by trials rushing upon him like wave upon wave in a stormy sea? Again the Saviour is nigh, and his gracious intimation, "It is I," produces a great calm.

Or is the believer perplexed, as if he were making no progress in the divine life, nay, were rather losing what he once thought he had acquired? "It is I," may reëncourage him, for He who utters these words will perfect what concerns us — He has undertaken for his people.

Is the believer drawing near to death, and do flesh and blood recoil? "It is I, be not afraid," revives his drooping spirit, and he enters the dark valley, perhaps with the song, "I will fear no evil."

Is conscience roused by the prospect of the

judgment? Has every sin a voice, and does every voice seem to exclaim, "The soul that sinneth shall die?" "It is I," uttered by Him whose blood cleanses us from all sin, may well reassure the troubled.

Does Satan pour in his fiery darts, and is this the keenest of them all? — What hope hast *thou*, thou, who hast sinned so long, so often, and so resolutely? This, from Him who is the Faithful witness. "It is I who can save to the uttermost," can at once quench the dart and quell the fear.

But when the archangel's trump shall sound, and the dead, small and great, shall stand before the Lord, how shall my soul encounter the glance of that eye which is like a flame of fire? "It is I," may invigorate even then; I who am your plea, I who am your Advocate, I who am your Judge.

It is thus that the Lord thinks upon us, and thus that, all along the path to glory, we may be animated to encounter every spiritual foe.

THE PROOF.

"Be not afraid of their terror, neither be troubled; but **sanctify the Lord God in your hearts**." — 1 Pet. iii. 14, 15.

THE HYMN.

"'It is I!' he exclaims, and I welcome my Lord,
 To soothe or to hush every fear;
'It is I!' and the waves which were raging **before**,
 Calm as infancy sleeping appear."

The Thoughts of Vanity.

"O JERUSALEM, WASH THINE HEART FROM WICKEDNESS, THAT THOU MAYEST BE SAVED: HOW LONG SHALL THY VAIN THOUGHTS LODGE WITHIN THEE?"—*Jer.* iv. 14.

IS not the Redeemer's remonstrance here one to which every soul should listen? Will not the holiest of the sons of men enter most profoundly into the words, "How long shall vain thoughts lodge within thee?"

It is a vain thought that I can do aught to merit the favor of God; and yet I am constantly cherishing it. I would come with a bridle in the one hand, and a boast in the other.

It is a vain thought that I can conquer sin in my own strength; and yet I constantly try it, that is, as often as I oppose sin at all; and hence my repeated disasters and falls.

It is a vain thought that I should repent first, and then come to Christ. But till I come to him, my very repentance is defiled. The true thought is, "He is exalted a prince and a Saviour for to *grant* repentance."

It is a vain thought that I can find rest, or any thing but tribulation here below, apart from God. The true thought is, "There remaineth a rest for the people of God."

It is a vain thought that I can prosper in the way of godliness without constant and assiduous prayer without making the Word of God the man of my right hand, and without recurring evermore for persevering grace, to Him whose converting grace first brought me to myself.

It is a very vain thought, and has proved the ruin of uncounted thousands, that we can be Christians without holiness, that is, followers of Christ without walking in his footsteps.

It is a vain thought, that I can do aught that is acceptable to God, without the prompting power of the Holy Ghost.

And, to name no more, it is a vain thought to think that I can be saved from perdition hereafter, unless I am saved from sin here.

Now, do these thoughts lodge within me? Then they must trouble my peace, they must impede my progress, and finally imperil my soul. But do I hate such thoughts of vanity? Do I pray for grace to "wash my heart from wickedness, that I may be saved?" Then the Lord is teaching. I glorify him for his grace, and because he is God and not man, such a soul will live before him.

THE PROOF.

"The thoughts of the righteous are right: but **the counsels of the wicked are deceit.**" — Prov. xii. 5.

THE WISH.

"Away, away, nor mar the peace
　The Holy Spirit sheds;
Why should the thoughts of vanity
　Bedim the bliss He spreads?"

The Effectual Prayer.

"LORD, REMEMBER ME WHEN THOU COMEST INTO THY KINGDOM." — *Luke* xxiii. 42.

IF this is not the most singular prayer ever uttered by mortal lips, it was uttered in the most singular circumstances and a most singular place — by the thief on the cross, an hour or two before the Redeemer carried him in triumph to glory, as a trophy of grace.

But that brief prayer, "Lord, remember me," has gladdened ten thousand times ten thousand and thousands of thousands of hearts since then. Enough for the believer to be just remembered by his Lord — there can be no lack, no disaster, no intolerable sorrow then. Lord, remember me when my heart and flesh do fail amid temptations. Lord, remember me when the enemy comes against me like a flood. Lord, remember me when those of my own household are my enemies or my plague. Lord, remember me when my own heart is threatening to betray me. Lord, remember me when sickness is pressing upon me, when friends desert me, when riches take to themselves wings and flee away. Lord, remember me when father and mother forsake me, when I am old and gray-headed, when I am near the swellings of Jordan, or when I enter the dark waters there. To be remembered by thee is enough. For that I plead, and except thou grant it, I will not let thee go!

He who asks in that spirit will not be refused. The answer to his prayer may not be, "This night shalt thou be with me in paradise;" but it will assuredly be this: "Where I am thou shalt be for ever, to follow the Lamb whithersoever he goes." That was a saying of singular condescension, "Concerning the work of my hands, *command ye Me*," and it is prayer which utters that command. He —

"Whose heart is made of tenderness,"

will refuse it nothing. Nay, he will "do as he has said," and teach even the most tried believer, who frequents the way to the throne of grace, to say —

"This is my favored lot —
My exaltation to afflictions high;
Afflicted I may be, it seems, and blest."

THE PROOF.

"Remember me, O Lord, with the favor that thou bearest unto thy people: O visit me with thy salvation; that I may see the good of thy chosen, that I may rejoice in the gladness of thy nation, that I may glory with thine inheritance." — PSALM cvi. 4, 5.

PRAYER.

"How blessed the Spirit who links to the throne
Where the soul's widest want is supplied;
How strong are the weak, how rich are the poor,
Who pray and trust God to provide?"

Strong in the Lord.

"BE STRONG IN THE LORD, AND IN THE POWER OF HIS MIGHT." — *Eph.* vi. 10.

THE Saviour of the lost, the brightness of the Father's glory, spoke of himself as a worm and no man: "But I am a worm, and no man; a reproach of men, and despised of the people"—so far did he humble himself in the work which God gave him to do. But that was only that his people might be exalted; and O what pains are taken to convince us of the strength which was made sure by the weakness and abasement of the Redeemer! "As thy day is, so shall thy strength be"—"My strength shall be perfected in thy weakness"—"Strengthened with all might in the inner man"—"He worketh all our works in us, and the work of faith with power"—"Unstable as water, we cannot excel," but "through Christ strengthening us we can do all things." These are some portions of Scripture which are designed to assure the believer of victory at the last. He cannot successfully resist a single temptation in his own strength. He cannot mortify a single sin. Even when he would do good, evil is present with him, and he is often forced to exclaim, "O wretched man that I am!" But still he has a perfect victory in reversion; he is even to be "more than a conqueror through Him who loved us." The worm Jacob is yet to thrash the mountains: "I will strengthen thee, yea, I will help thee," is the assurance of the mighty God of Jacob. "I will help thee, saith the Lord, and thy Redeemer the Holy One of Israel;" and then no weapon forged against us can prosper. The Lord is at our right hand, and who is he that can injure?

Now this may be the joy, as it is the safety of the timid soul. A weak faith can take hold of an Almighty arm, and then triumph in its strength. Were it not so, the strongest would faint and fail; but since it is so, the weakest may overcome, and sit down with the Saviour on his throne.

THE PROOF.

"Fear thou not; for I am with thee: be not dismayed; for I am thy God: I will strengthen thee: yea, I will help thee; yea, I will uphold thee with the right hand of my righteousness."— Isaiah xli. 10.

THE HYMN.

"From the sword at noon-day wasting
From the noisome pestilence,
At midnight thousands blasting,
Our God is our defence.

"Is there safety in omnipotence?
Is there peace in Salem's king?
Then hide thee, in thine impotence,
Beneath his sheltering wing."

The Lord alone Exalted.

"CHRIST IS ALL, AND IN ALL."—*Col.* iii. 11.

WERE it more habitually the aim of the believer to glorify his Lord, his peace would more speedily be like a mighty river; but as we seek rather to be saved than to see Christ glorified in our salvation, we are often disquieted and perplexed. In our very religion we are apt to become selfish; and if we escape from suffering and sorrow, the exaltation of the Saviour is too little contemplated. Now, in acting thus, we forsake our own mercies. True, the Holy one desires our salvation, and urges us to aim at it with heart and soul. Every motive which can rouse or stimulate us to that pursuit is employed. But to leave the Saviour's glory out of view, is plainly opposed to the will of God, and were it our aim that Christ may be magnified in our salvation; were it our desire that the Son of God should have the glory of saving the sons of men; were it our assiduous endeavor to make Christ all, and see him in all, then our salvation would be more surely promoted, while our happiness would be greater, for we should be more like-minded with the only wise God.

Is it so, then, that my soul has been aiming rather at salvation than at the glory of Christ in my salvation? In other words, have I been putting a part for the whole? Then let me cease to wonder that the Gospel has not yielded all the peace which it seems to promise. Nay, it could not yield it, for I have been mutilating the Gospel. But henceforth let me follow the Lord fully. Let Christ alone be exalted. Let me glory only in the Lord; and by that process — the process of divine appointment — I shall both fulfil the chief end of man, and delight myself in the abundance of peace.

There is a home which no enemy can enter, and which no friend will ever leave. The wicked cease from troubling there, and the weary are at rest. Now what is it that constitutes the blessedness of that abode? *Christ is there.* We believe in Him *here* as the Creator of all things, for "without Him was not any thing made;" as the Preserver of all, for "by Him all things consist;" and as the Redeemer of all who shall ever be saved. But *there* we shall see Him as he is, and our heaven would begin on this side the grave, did we but live for his glory, and rejoice when he is exalted.

THE PROOF.

"He is the head of the body, the church; who is the beginning, the first-born from the dead; that in all things he might have the preëminence." — COL. i. 18.

THE HYMN.

"In 'God with us,' my all I see,
My peace, my joy there shine —
All that I have or hope is his,
And naught but sin is mine."

Betrothed for Ever.

"THY MAKER IS THINE HUSBAND; THE LORD OF HOSTS IS HIS NAME; AND THY REDEEMER THE HOLY ONE OF ISRAEL; THE GOD OF THE WHOLE EARTH SHALL HE BE CALLED."—*Isaiah* liv. 5.

THIS is a promise to the church; but as the whole is composed of its parts, the assurance is as applicable to every individual soul as to the holy Catholic Church, the universal body of believers.

Thy Maker is thy husband, and he has betrothed thee unto him for ever. "I will betroth thee unto me for ever; yea, I will betroth thee unto me in righteousness, and in judgment, and in loving-kindness, and in mercies."

Thou mayest change,—it is in thine heart to forsake him from hour to hour; but he undertakes for thee, and therefore thou art safe. "For I am the Lord, I change not; therefore ye sons of Jacob are not consumed."

Thy vows would all be forgotten; thou wouldst turn from Him who alone can shelter, like the infatuated men around thee. But lest any one should hurt the soul, he will keep it with omniscient care. "I the Lord do keep it; I will water it every moment: lest any hurt it, I will keep it night and day."

Like the prodigal, thou wouldst become self-deceived and self-destroyed. But thy Maker is thy husband — He will defend; and only on that account art thou safe. "My Father, which gave them to me, is greater than all; and none is able to pluck them out of my Father's hand."

"The Lord of Hosts is his name;" on his strength therefore, the soul may lean and be sustained — "Thy Redeemer," and therefore may we stand fast, and rejoice in the liberty with which he makes free — "The Holy One of Israel," and therefore in holiness like his should the soul be arrayed from day to day. And lastly, "The God of the whole earth shall he be called." Behold the guaranty given to that soul whose Maker is its husband! He whose word commanded the universe to be — He whose will gives it law, and whose power continues to sustain it — is the strength and the stay of such a man. Should we not, then, be covered with shame, that any other lord should have dominion over us? And should this not be the firm resolution of every self-loving soul: "I will go and return to my first husband, for then it was better with me than now?"

THE PROOF

"I am my beloved's, and my beloved is mine." — Song vi. 2.

THE HYMN.

"I lean upon that mighty arm
  Which launched the worlds abroad,
And there I find my soul's defence,
  My Saviour and my God."

The Munition of Rocks.

"I WILL NOT BE AFRAID OF TEN THOUSANDS OF PEOPLE THAT HAVE SET THEMSELVES AGAINST ME ROUND ABOUT."— *Psalm* iii. 6.

WHAT need we fear, when the Lord Almighty is like walls and bulwarks round about us? What can hurt or offend, when the Lord's name is our strong tower into which we may run and be safe? Who is he that will injure, if the Lord of Hosts be on our side? If He who made the earth and the heavens, who stills the tumults of the people, and turns their fierceness into peace, be for us, who can be against us? The man after God's own heart was sometimes timid and dejected like other men: "I shall one day perish," was his conviction then, because he had forgotten who it is that upholds; his faith grew feeble, and he fell. But at other times, David was bold as a lion. "Why should such a man as I flee?"—"I will not be afraid of ten thousands of people"—"The Lord of Hosts is with us."—These, and such as these, were the holy man's confidence; and he could therefore "run through a troop" of opponents,

Now, in the one case, David is a beacon to warn us of danger; in the other, he is a model to be copied. There is danger in forgetting the Lord, as well as in forsaking him; and the moment that we forget him, we are tottering to our fall. But do we remember the years of the Most High? When the soul is overwhelmed and in perplexity, is it to the Rock that is higher than we that we flee? Then there is safety and a sure defence for us there. It may be with us as it was with Athanasius of old while he defended God's truth, and stood "alone against the world;" but though even that were the case—though we had not a single like-minded man with whom to take sweet counsel—He who keeps Israel would keep us like the apple of his eye.

It were wanton cruelty to lay a stumbling-block across the path of the blind. It would involve all the malignity of a murderer, to put poison in the wells of a city. But worse than that are they who would entice the soul away from the munition of rocks; who would tempt us to make God a liar, and rush against his buckler, instead of being sheltered by his shield. "Into their assembly, mine honor, be not thou united." Make Him thy sure defence, and live and die rejoicing.

THE PROOF.

"Ascribe ye greatness unto our God. He is the Rock, and his work is perfect."— DEUT. xxxii. 3, 4.

CONFIDENCE.

"When the surge of the ocean is foaming,
The rock laughs the fury to scorn;
And the soul which has sought the High Tower,
Far above every tempest is borne."

The Abased Exalted.

"I AM LESS THAN THE LEAST OF ALL SAINTS." — *Eph.* iii. 8.

LESS than the least! Is not that the language of extravagance or hyperbole? Could the apostle feel as he here says? Is it not exaggeration?

Such have been the views of some who knew not the Spirit who dwelt in Paul; but every child of God can, in some measure, enter into the apostle's meaning. If he might compare himself with the standards of earth, and be satisfied because he is like other sinners beside him, no such lowly confession would be heard. But the believer, whether in apostolic times or now, tests himself by the heavenly standard. It is a light matter for him to be judged of *man's* judgment; there is one that judgeth, even God. Perfection, therefore, is the model which the believer proposes; and hence his lowly confessions — hence his mouth is often in the dust. The further he ascends, he can just the more correctly measure what is still above him in the ascent. The holier he becomes, he is only enabled the more clearly to see the sinfulness of sin. The more Christlike any of the redeemed are made, the more accurate is their estimate of what nailed him to the tree. The more profound, therefore, are their convictions, the more assured do they feel that of all who are called saints, none so often grieve the Holy Spirit as they — they *know* at least of none. Hence their complaints; but, blessed be God, hence also may hope arise. The dead never complain! The outcry, then, is symptomatic of life; and as the holiest are always the humblest, so they are made glad by the assurance that God delights to dwell in the humble and the contrite heart. Be the dust, then, my bed; be sackcloth my covering; and, in the end, He that humbled will exalt. He may not take us as he took Amos, who was neither a prophet, nor a prophet's son, and say "Go prophesy unto my people." But are we conscious of guilt? Do we deplore it? Are we at the fountain, or on the way to it? Then He will not deal with us, as was the case with him who lay eight-and-thirty years by the pool. Nay, "Thy faith has made thee whole," will be the instant gladness of the soul.

THE PROOF.

"Thus saith the high and lofty One that inhabiteth eternity, whose name is Holy; I dwell in the high and holy place, with him also that is of a contrite and humble spirit, to revive the spirit of the humble, and to revive the heart of the contrite ones." — Isaiah lvii. 15.

THE HOPE.

"Low in the dust my soul should lie —
Is not the Spirit grieved?
Yet hope may spring, for lo, my God
Hath every want relieved."

The Great Contrast.

"AS SORROWFUL, YET ALWAY REJOICING; AS POOR, YET MAKING MANY RICH; AS HAVING NOTHING, AND YET POSSESSING ALL THINGS." — 2 *Cor.* vi. 10.

HOW mysterious does the Christian life, both in its joys and its sorrows, appear to the unconverted man!

In his joys the Christian is mysterious — for what do the unconverted know of the joy of the Lord, of joy in the Holy Ghost, of joy in believing, of the blessedness of the pardoned, or the fulness of joy which flows into the soul, when it is permitted to draw near to God, as its covenant God in Christ?

And in his sorrows as well as his joys, the believer is a riddle to the worldly man. The child of God mourns in his complaint and makes a noise, because of his shortcomings in prayer. The unconverted man either never prays, or a form is sufficient to soothe his conscience, like a soporific unto death.

The child of God is ceaselessly lamenting over the power of indwelling sin. The unconverted man is either unconscious of its existence, or turns it into mirth.

The child of God weeps in secret for the sins which abound, and rivers of waters run down his eyes, because men keep not God's commandments. But far from sorrowing for that, "fools make a mock at sin;" they scatter firebrands, arrows and death, yet say, Am not I in sport?

The child of God seeks to be saved from sin, and it is his sorrow to commit it, his joy to gain a victory over it: but keep an unconverted man from sinning, and you consign him prematurely to woe.

Now, if these things be so, how is it with thee, my soul? Is thy joy found in communion with God, in holiness, in dying to sin and living unto righteousness? Then the kingdom of God is within thee; the King of saints is reigning, and like the children of Zion, such souls may be joyful in their King. Sorrowful they may be over their condition on earth; poor they may be as regards this world's affluence, and unknown among its men; but they can joy in God, they are rich in faith, while the Lord knows their way. He guides them with his eye, and as the needle trembles and vibrates, with a sensibility like life, to the pole, so does that soul pant for God, the sun and the centre of its joy.

THE PROOF.

"We are troubled on every side, yet not distressed; we are perplexed, but not in despair."— 2 COR. iv. 8.

THE HYMN.

"Weeping, yet joyous; weak, yet mighty still;
Poor, yet enriching, is each humbled one;
Woe is his lot, while sin pollutes and plagues,
But joy unending waits him near the throne."

It is Well.

"ALL THESE THINGS ARE AGAINST ME." — *Gen.* xlii. 26.

SUCH is ever the conclusion of sense when it sits in judgment on the trials which the Holy One sends. Widowhood comes, because the creature was put in the Creator's place; and it is meant to win the heart to God. Poverty comes, and it is sent on the same errand. Long days and years of pining sickness are our lot, and the tried one mourns as if the Lord had forgotten to be gracious. But amid all these complaints, the very reverse of the believer's fears is true; for while man is faithlessly exclaiming, "All these things are against me," God is overruling them all, and they work together for good.

Was it not good that Joseph should be taken, when he was to stand at the right hand of royalty, and save a nation from famine and woe? Was it not good that Nebuchadnezzar should be bereft of his reason, and wander forth a roaming maniac, seeing that by that he was taught that the Most High God reigns? Was it not good that the Son of God should be laid in a grave, when from that grave, life and immortality were to spring? Was it not well that the infant church should be persecuted and scattered, when in consequence of that, the truth was to circulate throughout the world? He who sees the end from the beginning, does all things well; and could we learn, in humble confidence, to trust where we do not see, or to be silent when we cannot scan, sight as well as faith would at length be assured that just and true are all the ways of the King of saints. All that he does is done in wisdom, and goodness, and love.

Now, is my soul familiar with truth in this form? It is written in the word that "now abideth Faith, Hope, and Love"—do they abide in me?—Faith resting on the truth of God, Hope springing from faith, and Love, the flower or the fruit of all? Then may the soul rejoice in the house of its pilgrimage.

THE PROOF.

"We know that all things work together for good to them that love God, to them who are the called according to his purpose."— Rom. viii. 28.

THE HYMN.

"The darkening frown of Providence
  May gloom like thunder clouds;
But they break in showers of mercy
  On the soul which woe enshrouds.

"And though that soul in sorrow
  May faint beneath the rod,
Still, hope, like spring-tide gladdening,
  Will guide it to its God."

The Dew.

"I WILL BE AS THE DEW UNTO ISRAEL." — *Hos.* xiv. 5.

TO convey spiritual truth into the mind, the God of all grace has employed many figures which represent spiritual things to the very eye. Do we need a shelter? The Lord is our rock. Do we seek defence against our adversary? The Lord is our shield. Do we require something to gladden and refresh us? He is like rivers of water in a dry place. Do we sometimes sit in darkness and see no light? The Lord is a sun — He shines as the very Sun of Righteousness. Are we disconsolate? He is a Friend, a Father, a Brother. Are we parched and lifeless? He undertakes to be as the dew; and descending gently in silence, or "without observation," He spreads fertility and verdure where all would be sere and blighted. It is true, the dew may fall upon a rock, and nothing verdant will ever appear there; but not less true, that where He descends on ground which he has himself prepared, the fruit is unto holiness — thirty, sixty, or an hundred-fold — the promise is fulfilled, "He shall grow as the lily, and cast forth his roots like Lebanon."

My soul! Is the Lord all this to thee? Is it true that he has come to gladden thee as the dew the green herb? And hast thou, like the little flower, drunk in that dew so as to be invigorated like the tree planted by the rivers of water? Then give Him the glory; and O, see that the fruit be abundant, and more abundant still.

But has the Lord been to thee like waters that fail? Then why? Has he broken his promise, or hast thou refused to believe it? Has he proved untrue, or art thou detected to be faithless? Has he reversed the saying, "The gifts and calling of God are without repentance," or hast thou listened to the evil heart of unbelief, and not to Him who is the truth? If so, then return and do thy first works. Wait on the Lord, but wait in faith, and "They that wait upon the Lord shall renew their strength; they shall mount up on wings like eagles; they shall run and not be weary; and walk and not faint." "The shower upon the grass that waiteth not for man, nor tarrieth for the sons of men," will descend upon the soul.

THE PROOF.

"The righteous shall flourish like the palm-tree; he shall grow like a cedar in Lebanon." — PSALM xcii. 12.

THE HYMN.

"Gentle as dew to gladden,
　The grace of the Holy One;
And sweet as the rose of Sharon,
　The blood shed to atone."

Prayer: its Power.

"BEFORE THEY CALL, I WILL ANSWER; AND WHILE THEY ARE YET SPEAKING, I WILL HEAR."— *Isaiah* lxv. 24.

WHAT vital air is to animal life, prayer is to spiritual existence. As well may the body of man attempt to live in the caves of the ocean, as his soul to prosper without intercourse with God.

How blessed, then, that God is specially revealed as the hearer of prayer! It is like one of his attributes, to listen to the supplications of his people; and precept, promise, example, lesson — all that divine wisdom can devise, or divine truth guarantee, or divine mercy make good, is put upon record, to encourage us to pray. Yea, so much is the heart of God set on hearing our petitions, that He actually undertakes to hear us before we call. The first dawning wish is marked. The most incipient desire is noted. Before our words have embodied the thoughts of our heart, the Hearer of prayer has heard them in our breast. Nay, it is himself that prompts the desire, the wish, the prayer; for He pours out upon us the Spirit of grace and supplications. He teaches us to pray; or, more amazing still, as the "Man of Sorrows," he sets us the example of prayer — whole nights are spent in the privilege! He is thereby braced for agony, and strengthened for the death-struggle with every foe of his people.

So must it be with thee, my soul, or thou wilt perish from the way! "Praying always with all prayer and supplication;" "Pray without ceasing;" "Ye people, pour ye out your hearts before him;" "Will the hypocrite pray always?"— These are some portions of the Word by which the God of pardons would encourage or stimulate us to approach him; and they are greatly blessed who have caught that spirit, and cannot be long from the throne. To hang upon God, to wait for his blessing, to enjoy communion with him, to have every gift sweetened by the thought that it is in answer to prayer — is not that heaven begun, a foretaste of the fulness of joy? One of the strangest portions of the Word of God has reference to this subject — that which tells us to " *Give God no rest:*" "And give him no rest, till he establish, and till he make Jerusalem a praise in the earth;" and happy is the man whom the Holy Spirit teaches to act on the amazing injunction! O my soul, act thou upon it, and so be blessed and made a blessing.

THE PROOF.

"O thou that hearest prayer, unto thee shall all flesh come." — Psalm lxv. 2.

THE HYMN.

"Would the weary soul soar away from its woes?
Be prayer its wings, and Jehovah its rest;
Would the sinner escape from the crimson stain?
Let the prayer of faith seek the Saviour's breast."

The Saviour's Kindred.

"WHOSOEVER SHALL DO THE WILL OF MY FATHER WHICH IS IN HEAVEN, THE SAME IS MY BROTHER, AND SISTER, AND MOTHER." — *Matt.* xii. 50.

MARK how it is that we can prove ourselves to be the members of the household of faith. Not merely by a correct creed, important as that is. Not by a mere profession. Not by holding a religion which is deposited in a book and left there, like any of the records of the past deposited in our archives. But by abounding in holy deeds. By doing the will of Christ's God and our God, Christ's Father and our Father. Holiness to the Lord is to be our constant aim, and if we neglect it, we are destitute of the family likeness; the first-born of many brethren does not own or recognize us. "This is the will of God, even our sanctification." — Now, is that will of God ours? Then the Shepherd of Israel has taught us that we are his spiritual kindred, the "members of his body, of his flesh, and of his bones." But is the will of God opposed by us? Is sanctification not sought, watched for, striven for, prayed for? Then we are none of his, and the day is coming when all will be unmasked before the universe assembled.

Be it my endeavor, then, my prayer, my ever earnest aim, to grow in holiness. Let every day be deemed a lost one in which I do not grow somewhat more like God's "holy child Jesus." In that spirit, God will make me a conqueror. He will not save me *for my holiness* — He will save me only *for Christ.* But holiness is itself a part of my salvation; I am thereby prepared for that abode which nothing that defiles can enter; and he is a partaker of the divine nature who is learning this holy science. Christ-likeness is thus the consummation of redemption.

That was a wondrous charge brought against the Jews of old, when it was said that they were "*A comfort to Sodom.*" People of God as they were, and signalized by ten thousand mercies, they yet cheered and countenanced the wicked in their ways, till the most abandoned of the sons of men found a shelter for their profligacy behind the example of the chosen people. Is there no danger that that woful case may be repeated still? O, let me watch and pray, lest my example cheer the godless on the way to ruin.

THE PROOF.

"We all with open face beholding as in a glass the glory of the Lord, are changed into the same image, from glory to glory even as by the Spirit of the Lord." — 2 Cor. iii. 18.

THE HYMN.

"Bless the Lord, O my soul, for the Saviour's work,
    And not less for the hallowing One;
If Jesus admits the lost soul to the skies,
    His Spirit prepares for the throne."

The Hope of Glory.

"HE THAT BELIEVETH ON ME HATH EVERLASTING LIFE."
—*John* vi. 47.

THE believer does not need to wait till eternity begin before he enjoy his blessings. Though the world deems them distant, and shadowy, and dim, and therefore despises them all, the Christian knows that there is a present pardon, a present peace, a present joy, prepared for us, and actually possessed. The secret of the Lord is with them that fear him; he shows them his covenant; he lays open his mind; and as this is the accepted time, it is also the time when that blessedness of a believer which is to endure for ever, begins to be enjoyed.

The Saviour therefore says, "He that believeth on me *hath* everlasting life." It has already begun. A vital principle which death cannot touch, is already animating that frame in which "a kingdom which cannot be moved" is already set up. Light is not merely sown for the righteous to grow hereafter; it is already enjoyed. He walks in it. In short, a present salvation, a present peace, a present repose in God — foretastes of the fulness of joy, convictions that "My Redeemer liveth" — all these and countless more, are the fruits of the Spirit in the soul; and he is blessed of the Lord who made the heavens and the earth, who has opened his heart to Him, who stands and knocks that he may enter now, and bring in his train these foretastes of the fulness of joy, the pleasures which are for evermore. Christ is thus formed in us the hope of glory. He himself is the life, and neither death nor the grave can obscure or eclipse it.

But, O, how strange that these things are often so dim, and unsubstantial even to the believer in Jesus! They seem like the honeycomb when robbed of its sweetness, or wells without water, and clouds without rain, but the change is in the believer, not in them. The world has been decoying — sin has been tampered with — or the evil heart of unbelief consulted; and under the saddening conviction of that, the soul illumined from heaven, may gather joy from the assurance that its hopes repose on one who is "the same yesterday, to-day, and forever."

THE PROOF.

"Behold the kingdom of God is within you." — LUKE xvii. 21.
"The kingdom of God is righteousness and peace, and joy in the Holy Ghost." — ROM. xiv. 17.

THE HYMN.

"Above every woe which harasses the heart
 The believer in Jesus may rise:
He has glory and honor immortal in store,
 And may patiently wait for the skies."

v*

The Heavenly-Minded.

"OUR CONVERSATION IS IN HEAVEN."—*Phil.* iii. 20.

THERE is a family on the eve of emigration, and mark how assiduous they are in preparing. They have made inquiry in every available quarter, and through every open channel. Their heart is already in the land of their adoption; at least the ties which link them to the land of their fathers are gradually weakened. This one has been broken — that other is in course of being loosened. The whole will soon be snapt, and all will embark for what is deemed a better country.

Now, we seek a heavenly country; and should not our thoughts be often sent on before us? Should not our affections be there? Should we not seek to have our treasures transported thither, as the Spirit of God directs the spiritual mind? And it is so with the Christian indeed, according to the mind of his Lord. He has his affections set on things above. His conversation is in heaven. It is often on his lips, and oftener in his heart. He loves to dwell on the blessedness of the New Jerusalem, the city of our God, and has his solemn seasons set apart for cherishing that joy. He remembers that there was a time when even his religion was too much set on things below, nay, it is often so still; but he feels that that is his infirmity — his sin — and he now cultivates that heavenly-mindedness which is life and peace. He has treasures in heaven, and his heart is also there. He seeks first the kingdom of God and his righteousness, and as the mountain-tops are both the first to see and the last to reflect the sun, so the hoary head sometimes reflects some rays of the coming heaven: the song of the dying sometimes is — " Henceforth there is laid up for me a crown of glory which fadeth not away."

Let me cultivate heavenly-mindedness. Let me remember that I am a pilgrim and a stranger. O. let my heart be set on things above, where Christ sits at God's right hand. That is life and peace; and when the closing scene draws on, all else will be seen to have been only mockery — a shadow or a dream.

THE PROOF.

"Seek ye first the kingdom of God and his righteousness; and all these things shall be added unto you." — MATT. vi. 33.

THE CONVICTION.

" By the blest fountain of his blood,
   My soul first found its peace;
And when the life is hid in God,
   That joy shall never cease.

" The mirage mocks the pilgrim's eye;
   The moon's pale beam is chill;
But living streams, and radiant suns
   That soul with **gladness fill**."

The Crown.

"IT DOTH NOT YET APPEAR WHAT WE SHALL BE."—1 *John* iii. 2.

WE walk by faith. We are only in our minority here. We are still but in the outer court; only our Forerunner, and the spirits of the just made perfect, have as yet entered the Holy of Holies; and, till we be there, we cannot comprehend the nature of our future existence, or our future home: it is dark with excess of light. But one thing we know: Christ will be there—we shall be like him, and see him as he is; and that is heaven enough to the soul which has been washed in the Redeemer's blood, and saved by the Redeemer's power, and transformed by the Redeemer's Spirit—there is amply enough in that to allure us to the skies. It will be

"An over-payment of delight,"

for all the ills, and self-denial, or self-sacrifice of a believer's life, to be for ever with the Lord—for ever like Him, and to be led by Him to the green pastures on the holy mountain, where there is nothing to hurt or to offend.

Arise, then, my soul, from the dust, and cease to grovel like the imbruted, or like those who are laden with thick clay. Live like an heir of God, a joint-heir with Christ. Never forget that the day of thy death is to be the day of thy coronation. Be like those who know that they are the heirs of a kingdom which shall not be moved; and surely you may joyfully endure as seeing Him who is invisible, when you know so well that tribulation is the path to glory.

Is it not strange that man has so completely reversed the order of God as to put the shadow for the substance, time for eternity, the transient for the enduring, the human for the divine? We walk among shadows, and yet persist in deeming them realities; we listen to empty echo, and trust it more than the truth of God; in a word, the way of wisdom is turned upside down. But he who sits in heaven proclaims, "Behold, I make all things new," and the new heart looks for the new heavens and the new earth wherein righteousness is to dwell. Faith turns them into actual realities (Heb. xi. 1), and the soul already rejoices.

THE PROOF.

"Henceforth there is laid up for me a crown of righteousness, which the Lord, the righteous Judge, shall give me at that day; and not to me only, but unto all them also that love his appearing."—2 Tim. iv. 8.

THE HYMN.

"It sparkles to the eye of faith,
   You glorious crown in heaven;
As if two suns were shining there,
   On those God has forgiven."

Heavenward Progress.

"GROW IN GRACE, AND IN THE KNOWLEDGE OF OUR LORD AND SAVIOUR JESUS CHRIST. TO HIM BE GLORY BOTH NOW AND FOR EVER. AMEN."—2 *Pet.* iii. 18.

ALL the fulness of the Godhead dwells bodily in Jesus, and yet, O how little of his glory do the holiest know! We see some far-off glimpses of it; we hear some echoes; we touch the hem of his garment, and from time to time the Spirit-taught soul would stoop to unloose the latchet of his shoe. Yet years roll on years, while we know little of him but the name. We call him "God with us," but feel little of his power. We reckon him "the chief among ten thousand," but often overlook his beauty. We know that he has "the fulness of joy," and yet we often sit in sackcloth. We droop and pine, even though he undertakes to keep us night and day, lest any one should hurt us.

But it is his mind that we should grow in the knowledge of him — of his power at once to cleanse us from the pollution of sin, and to free us from its dominion; to bring us nearer and nearer to the long-lost image of God; to restore happiness to the disconsolate, and holiness to the sinful, and heaven to those who had forfeited it for ever. Instead of being satisfied merely with the knowledge of his name, we should know him more and more from day to day. The power of his resurrection, his glory in the church, his suitableness *to us*, his deep sympathy, his unquenchable love to man, should all be more and more felt, or become more and more attractive, and that soul is prospering — it is happy, it is blessed indeed — which is thus growing in the knowledge of our Lord and Saviour. He is our hiding-place — Do I know Him in that character? Our peace — is he felt to be so? Our all — is that the soul's conviction, and is it more and more felt as days and years sweep past? Then the Spirit of grace is guiding, and grace will anon be glory.

Nor let the soul fail to notice that our God means us to rejoice. Not gloom, not sackcloth, not bondage and terror; but light and beauty, hope and freedom should signalize the child of God. "That your joy may be full," is again and again recorded as the design of God regarding his people, and that joy is made sure by spiritual progress.

THE PROOF.

"Add to your faith, virtue; and to virtue, knowledge; and to knowledge, temperance; and to temperance, patience; and to patience, godliness; and to godliness, brotherly kindness; and to brotherly kindness, charity." — 2 Pet. i. 5-7

THE HYMN.

"God's saints from strength unwearied go,
  Still onward unto strength;
Until in Zion they appear,
  Before the Lord at length."

The Second Adam.

"AS WE HAVE BORNE THE IMAGE OF THE EARTHY, WE SHALL ALSO BEAR THE IMAGE OF THE HEAVENLY."—1 *Cor.* xv. 49.

IN the soul which grovels in the dust, and seeks a portion among things which perish in the using, it is difficult to realize the noble destiny for which man was at first created. The diamond buried deep in the earth, or precious merchandise sunk by shipwreck in the ocean, does not seem more completely beyond our reach, than purity and dignity appear to have passed for ever away from that degraded soul.

But he who created can create anew. He who saw the fall can lift us from it; and though we have sunk so low, that nearly every trace of our primal dignity is effaced, yet he who adorned man's soul with beauty at first can re-adorn it; and that is the process through which every child of God is passing. The second Adam, the Lord from heaven, appears among the sons of men, to retrieve the ruin wrought by the first. His voice addresses men in accents of mercy; and do they hear when he calls? Then the grand transforming process has begun. Walking with Jesus in newness of life, that soul will grow like him, and liker still, even till the image of God be restored, and that which is perfect be come. Sorrow and joy, disappointment and success, seasons of sunshine and nights of weeping, will all be blessed by the Spirit of grace to promote that end; and as the sculptor, by slow degrees, evolves a form of exquisite beauty from some rude block, the new-creating Spirit traces line upon line in the heart of man, till the beauty of holiness be there again. Now, that is the joy of the soul; that is its healthy and vigorous condition. It was diseased, deformed, and offensive once; it is now made like its God again, and joyously anticipates the time, or rather the eternity, when it shall see no more darkly as in a glass, but face to face, knowing as it is known, and perfect for ever in all the will of God.

THE PROOF.

"And so it is written, the first man Adam was made a living soul, the last Adam was made a quickening spirit."—1 COR. XV. 45.

THE HYMN.

"The fiat which bade Adam be,
 To crown creation here below,
Seemed vain, when Adam dared to sin,
 And plunge his race in hopeless woe.

"But hark! another fiat still
 Peals like an anthem from the skies —
The second Adam stoops to earth,
 And bids us from our ruin rise.

"Lo! beauty now where all was marred;
 See joy where all was woe before;
See God once more enthroned by man;
 Hear ransomed crowds that God adore."

Transgression Finished.

"FOR I WILL BE MERCIFUL TO THEIR UNRIGHTEOUSNESS, AND THEIR SINS AND THEIR INIQUITIES WILL I REMEMBER NO MORE."—*Heb.* viii. 12.

WHAT is it that makes man dread God? It is sin. What is it that makes man at one time recoil in terror from death, and at another madly court it? It is sin. What is it that wrings tears from our eyes, and groans from our heart; that often banishes hope, and leaves man a prey to torment before the time? It is sin. And what is it that often erects the tribunal of God, with such blackness and darkness, before the guilty conscience? It is sin. What, then, is needed to give man hope? What can encourage him amid the woes of earth, or the yet more appalling ordeal of death, and the judgment which follows it? It is an assurance from the lips of the Judge, that sin shall be for ever put away.

And is it not, then, like a glimpse of the blessedness of heaven, to hear him say, "I will be merciful to their unrighteousness, and their sins and their iniquities will I remember no more?" The troubled conscience may now have peace, if it will come to God upon his own terms. The aching heart may now be soothed, if it will glorify God as the God of pardons in Christ. The soul which has perhaps felt as if there were nothing before it but the blackness of darkness for ever, may at length joy in God through Him whose blood is the fountain of hope, and "O that men would praise the Lord for this goodness, and these wonderful works to the children of men!" The soul just awakened to solemn thought, and the soul which has walked, perhaps for half a century, in the good ways of the Lord, alike need a pardon. Both at the commencement and the close of a holy life, that is the great desideratum of the earnest spirit; and blessed are they whom the Holy One has taught to understand and to feel, that "there is forgiveness with God that he may be feared"—a forgiveness free, instantaneous, and complete to the chief of sinners, the moment they believe.

O cleave, my soul, to that, even on the eve of quitting the frail body, and leaving it to the worm and the grave. Sins are countless; guilt is heavy; but the blood of Christ cleanses from it all. A few more months, or days, or breaths, and through almighty grace, thou art pure as Christ is pure, for ever.

THE PROOF.

"If we confess our sins, he is faithful and just to forgive us our sins, and to cleanse us from all unrighteousness."—1 JOHN i. 9.

THE HYMN.

"The crowding woes which crush the heart of man,
  And shroud his future in a rayless gloom,
Might goad to frenzy, had not God, in love,
  Sent forth the Victim who averts our doom."

The Triumph.

"I AM IN A STRAIT BETWIXT TWO, HAVING A DESIRE TO DEPART, AND TO BE WITH CHRIST; WHICH IS FAR BETTER."— *Phil.* i. 23.

FAITH is that grace which gives substance to what the world deems a shadow, and guided by faith, the child of God sometimes longs to be away to his Father's home, the house of the Lord, for ever. Here he groans, being burdened. He carries about with him a load of sin, and escape from it he cannot, however he may pine, and pray, and watch, and strive. He knows, however, that that which is perfect is coming. He knows, moreover, that the ransomed of the Lord are to be with him for ever, to see him as he is, to be like Him who makes all things new; in short, saved alike from sin in itself, and sin in all its consequences. For that, then, the believer hungers and thirsts. To him at least, heaven is a reality; its joys and its purities are substantial and abiding, nay, the only substantial and abiding things; and it will be the day of his soul's coronation, when all these are put in his possession, to fill his heart to overflowing for ever.

It is not an escape merely from the woes, the bondage, and the tears of earth, that a believer seeks; these he will endure as long as his God appoints; but his desire to depart originates in the strong craving of his regenerated soul to be for ever with his Lord, and be satisfied when he awakes in his likeness. The Alpha of his hopes becomes their Omega, when his foot is on the threshold of glory — Now my soul, is this thy crowning desire? In thy brighter moments at least, are thy longing aspirations directed to the Lord of Glory, as thy chief and thine eternal good? Then go on thy way rejoicing. All things are thine, for the Lord of all is thine; and when the mirage of life shall have melted away, the everlasting habitations will be thy home, and thy God thy glory. Thou art incapable of enjoying more than that, and the God of all grace has not provided less.

THE PROOF.

"According to his promise, we look for new heavens and a new earth, wherein dwelleth righteousness." — 2 Pet. iii. 13.

THE HYMN.

"As travellers oft in deserts hail
   The distant mirage, and rejoice,
Deluded man is oft decoyed
   By pleasure's soft and syren voice.

"And as these travellers faint the more,
   When that mirage melts all away,
So chafed and woe-worn man must weep,
   When he and hope alike decay.

"But see the land of Beulah rise,
   Mark rolling there the streams of life;
O wake, my soul, and grasp the joys
   Which close thy weary mortal strife."

Death Abolished.

"AND ALL THE DAYS OF METHUSELAH WERE NINE HUNDRED SIXTY AND NINE; AND HE DIED." — *Gen.* v. 27.

SUCH is the solemn, dirge-like close of the record of a life which lasted nearly a thousand years — such is the solemn, dirge-like close of the life of every child of Adam — of Adam's universal race "And he died." But O, who will tell what is implied in death! To leave all the warm realities of earth! — to break up its countless ties, and launch into a vast and dark unknown! — to be laid in the place of skulls and skeletons! — to say to the worm, Thou art my mother, and thou art my sister! Then to meet the Judge upon the great white throne! to be confronted with Him, and with every sin we ever committed, unless it be washed away in the blood of the Redeemer! And, finally, to hear the terrific words, Depart ye accursed! or the gladdening ones, Enter on the joy of your Lord! Who has conceived it? Who can picture it? Who, in his own strength, can meet the great and terrible day of the Lord?

But He himself prepares us for meeting it. He is our life — He is our Advocate — He is our righteousness — He is our resurrection. Death must do its work on the body, but it is powerless against the soul. In Christ we live, and are alive for **ever** more; and may begin, even amid the shadows of earth, the believer's triumphal song: "O death, where is thy sting? O grave, where is thy victory?" I see a land where there shall be no more death — where Christ liveth; and because he liveth, we shall live also.

He died — that man who lived oblivious of God

He died — that man who made evil his good.

He died — that man who refused to listen to God's beseeching voice from the cross of his Son.

He died — that man who was once a professed believer, but saw cause to trample under foot the blood of the covenant.

He died — that simple-minded believer in Christ, that temple of the Holy Spirit.

And *I must die* — to which class do I belong?

THE PROOF.

"Jesus Christ .... hath abolished death, and hath brought life and immortality to light through the gospel." — 2 Tim. i. 10.

THE TRIUMPH.

" Death, the last foe, is vanquished now,
   The Life has robbed the grave;
And fadeless crowns are round the brow
   Of all he came to save.

" Hosanna from the ransomed raise
   To David's Lord and Son;
Immortals, haste, the Saviour praise!
   For he your glories won."

Following the Lamb.

"THE LAMB, WHICH IS IN THE MIDST OF THE THRONE SHALL FEED THEM, AND SHALL LEAD THEM UNTO LIVING FOUNTAINS OF WATERS; AND GOD SHALL WIPE AWAY ALL TEARS FROM THEIR EYES." — *Rev.* vii. 17.

THE Lamb is not merely the sinner's hope on earth, but moreover, the ransomed spirit's joy in glory — never for a moment are our thoughts permitted to wander from him. As the close of his pilgrimage draws near, the believer rejoices in the prospect of following the Lamb for ever, whithersoever he goes. Like the weary exile approaching the land of his fathers, and eager the more as he draws nearer to its shores, that believer at times longs to depart and be with Jesus. Does sin harass him? He thinks of the Lamb of God who takes it all away, and remembers that, even in regard to glory, a vision once showed a lamb as it had been slain. Or does the believer, as he draws nearer to the close of his earthly career, anticipate deliverance from the woes of earth? It is because the Lamb in the midst of the throne is to welcome him there. In a word, glory just consists in following the Lamb of God, and being for ever with him; delighting in the blessings which he purchased, and which, *as his purchase,* it is the heaven of the redeemed to enjoy.

Now, is my soul preparing for that **glory?** Is

there no mistake, no assumption, no danger of self-deception? Nothing that defiles can enter there. Have I, then, washed my robes, and made them pure in the blood of the Lamb? There is no woe beyond the grave to those who, on this side, behold the Lamb. Have I, then, seen him, and rejoiced? Lamb though he be, he is mighty to save; and none but him can deliver. Is it there, then, that I repose? In a word, is the heaven for which I live, the heaven of the Lamb of God, where He will lead, and guide, and bless, world without end? Then those whom I love may drop into the grave, and leave me only tears in their stead — those in whom I confide may prove false — those for whom I pray and watch may pierce me through with many sorrows; but just the more should the soul rejoice in the Lamb of God. In the fulness of time, he will "wipe away all tears from all eyes."

THE PROOF.

"These are they which follow the Lamb whithersoever he goeth. These were redeemed from among men, being the first fruits unto God and to the Lamb."—REV. xiv. 4.

THE HYMN.

"Worthy the Lamb that died, they cry,
  To be exalted thus;
Worthy the Lamb, let us reply,
  For he was slain for us.

"To him be power divine ascribed,
  And endless blessings paid;
Salvation, glory, joy, remain
  For ever on his head!"

Heaven.

"THEM ALSO WHICH SLEEP IN JESUS WILL GOD BRING WITH HIM."—1 *Thess.* iv. 14.

THIS is the conclusion of the whole matter. Death is abolished; the body is raised; and with soul and body re-united, we are to be for ever with the Lord. The almighty power which brought Jesus from the dead is to bring us with him. Death is robbed of its terrors by the Lord of life, and now seems only a sleep; reposing in Jesus, we are to rise with him who is the first fruits from the dead. Our very dust is part of his redeemed property. He died to rescue it from the pollution of sin, and the power of the grave; and thus to be for ever with the Lord, is now the destiny of the believer, in soul and in body.

May we not, then, already begin to exult? Is not the cope-stone put upon the plan of redemption? Is not grace proved to be the bud of glory? Is not the soul just passing from woe to blessedness? Is not Christ indeed the life? Are not all the sufferings of earth proved to be what God says they are — not worthy to be compared with the glory which is to be revealed? Prepare, my soul, for all that glory. Faith will soon be sight. Holiness will soon supersede all pollution, and what you now see darkly as in a glass, will soon be seen face to face. Christ will soon be absolutely all in all, and thou shalt soon be absolutely and for ever like him. That is heaven — the consummation of the Father's love, of the Redeemer's agony, and the Spirit's work.

To be with Christ — Behold the copestone of a believer's desire, the terminating point of all his aspirations! That implies entire and eternal freedom from sin, alike in its condemning, its enslaving, and polluting power. In the resurrection-state, the ransomed soul is perfectly like the Holy, Harmless, Sinless One. Whether its life on earth has been like that of the lowland stream,

"Dimpling along in silent majesty,"

or, like the mountain torrent,

"Tearing its way amid a thousand crags,"

the end is the same — to be through grace for ever with the Lord, and for ever like Him.

THE PROOF.

"But now is Christ risen from the dead, and become the first fruits of them that slept."—1 COR. xv. 20.

THE HYMN.

"Hosanna! the sepulchre hears the loud peal;
 Lo! the blood-ransomed millions arise;
 And clothed in the robes which the Ransomer wove,
 With him they are scaling the skies."

www.ingramcontent.com/pod-product-compliance
Lightning Source LLC
Chambersburg PA
CBHW031932230426
43672CB00010B/1896